Herbs &
Edible Flowers

Easy Plants for More Beautiful Gardens

Produced by Storey Communications, Inc.
Pownal, Vermont

Library of Congress Cataloging-in-Publication Data is available.
ISBN 0-395-87335-5

Printed in the United States of America

WCT 10 9 8 7 6 5 4 3 2 1

CONTENTS

INTRODUCTION

Of the many types of plants that grow in our gardens, herbs hold a very special place. For centuries, we have studied them, grown them, and used them. Humanity, it seems, cultivated herbs even before it cultivated civilization. In short, herbs have been our partners for a very long time.

People have used herbs to heal their bodies, calm their minds, add fragrance to their homes, and flavor and preserve their foods. They have been used to stuff mattresses, repel pests, and attract butterflies and birds to soothe our spirits. Herbs improve the quality of our lives. In a world as fast-paced as ours, this is, indeed, a very special contribution.

Herbs as Magic

The value of herbs has never been questioned by the societies that used them. However, just how they accomplish their myriad wonders has been a mystery through the ages. For generations, science was not sophisticated enough to reveal the secrets of herbs. Lacking the scientific answers, people devised magical ones instead.

To the Egyptians, the onion was sacred; they believed that the layers of the bulb symbolized the different layers of the universe. Herbs were used to prepare the bodies of deceased pharaohs for their afterlife journey and to decorate their resting places. In ancient Greece, sweet bay was considered much more than a plant. This warm, spicy herb was regarded as the transformed nymph Daphne, who offered herself to the people as sweet bay to escape the unwanted advances of the god Apollo.

To other peoples, such as the Jews of the Middle East, herbs were considered medicines harvested from the earth by humans, but created and endowed with their curative powers by God.

Finding Answers

Today, modern science has replaced the magic and mystery of herbs with logic and reason. The compounds and chemicals responsible for the many attributes of herbs are slowly but surely coming to light. The burning spiciness of hot peppers, the relaxing aroma of lavender, the soothing quality of chamomile—these and many other qualities of herbs have come under close scrutiny. Not surprisingly, many of the folk remedies and ancient uses ascribed to herbs have been validated by modern science. Hot peppers are still used to relieve pain, as they have been for hundreds of years; lavender still helps people get a good night's sleep; and chamomile is a favorite home remedy for an upset stomach. Science has cast a different light on our partnership with herbs, an illumination that continues to validate the importance and versatility of these wonderful plants.

All the Best

This guide is a compendium of the most useful herbs commonly grown today—our best herb-garden partners. The plants are arranged alphabetically by scientific name, with the common name in large type just above the scientific one. Each plant is identified with a large photograph accompanied by an at-a-glance box with a brief list of important features, including plant hardiness, type and size, identifying characteristics, and the plant's principal uses. An introduction acquaints you with the herb's special attributes.

In "How to Grow" you'll find the necessary cultural techniques as well as the conditions required, such as the best type of soil, directions for watering, and maintenance techniques specific to the featured herb. The best method of propagation is also highlighted in this section—you'll know whether to sow seeds, take cuttings, or divide the plant to grow additional plants.

Following the growing information, you'll find the most common uses of the herb. Here the parts of the plant and their common uses are identified. Harvesting and storage techniques are included, along with methods of preparation. The colorful sidebar to the right contains tips and techniques to enhance your enjoyment of the plant.

When available, a list of varieties with special merit, called "Top Choices," is also included. The unique qualities of each recommended plant are described there, so that you can easily choose those that meet your herb-gardening requirements.

At your fingertips, you have all the information you need to get started in herb gardening and to learn how to use and enjoy herbs all year long.

ANISE HYSSOP
Agastache foeniculum

Zones: 4–8

Type: Perennial

Light: Full sun or part shade

Size: 4 ft. tall, 2 ft. wide

Interest: Nectar-rich, red-purple flower spikes that attract bees, butterflies, and hummingbirds

Uses: Culinary, cut flowers, decorative, medicinal

Dense spikes of 3-inch-long, rose-violet blooms top the stiff upright stems of this neat, sweetly scented perennial. Anise hyssop stems have four sides, like other members of the mint family. Its common names—anise hyssop, blue giant hyssop, and fennel giant hyssop—derive from the plant's sweet licorice fragrance and similar appearance to hyssop, another member of the mint family. The soft, pointed leaves are flushed with purple in early spring and turn bright green by the time the plants are fully grown.

HOW TO GROW
This pest-free herb is native to the North American prairies and thrives in average, well-drained soil in full sun to light shade. Too much shade or nitrogen fertilizer often produces a floppy plant that requires staking.

Sow seeds or transplant self-sown seedlings in spring. Divide in fall from Zone 7 south, and spring elsewhere. To keep the plant from increasing too rapidly, snip off the blossoms before they can produce seeds.

HOW TO USE

The purple flower spikes of anise hyssop make lovely cut flowers and look handsome in a vase with other summer blooms. The dried flowers and leaves can be added to potpourri or used to make a refreshing anise-flavored tea. The fresh leaves and flowers are a spicy addition to salads and make a tea with a slightly sharper flavor than do dried leaves alone. The flowers add color and flavor to fruit pies, or try them with other edible flowers for a pretty garnish.

Top Choices

- *A. foeniculum* 'Alabaster' has spikes of creamy white flowers and grows 2 feet tall and 1 foot wide.

- *A.* x 'Firebird' has aromatic leaves on 2-foot stems topped with spikes of rust-orange flowers.

- *A.* x 'Tutti Fruti' has strong 2-foot stems and burgundy blossoms.

- *A. rugosa*, Korean mint, grows 5 feet tall and 2 feet wide. Minty, aromatic leaves and spikes of purple flowers are characteristic. Zones 6 to 9.

AIR DRYING ANISE HYSSOP

To air-dry anise hyssop for use in tea or potpourri:

1 Cut stems, tie the base ends together with string, and hang upside down in a warm, dry space out of direct light.

2 To keep the bunch dust-free, place it in a brown paper bag punched with ventilation holes. Leaves usually take from five to seven days to dry.

3 When crumbly dry, remove the leaves and flowers from the stems and store them in an air-tight glass jar.

4 Store the jar in a cool, dry, dark place until ready to use.

The attractive blossoms of anise hyssop make it welcome in the perennial border as well as the herb garden.

HOLLYHOCK
Alcea rosea

Zones: 4–9

Type: Biennial or
short-lived perennial

Light: Full sun

Size: 4–8 ft. tall,
up to 2 ft. wide

Interest: Tall spikes of
large flowers in every
color but blue

Uses: Culinary,
decorative

These tall, stately plants have long had a traditional place at the back of the border or herb garden. During their first year, the plants produce a low clump of rough foliage. The following year, each plant develops three to six strong stalks that reach up to 8 feet tall. Each stem is studded with buds that open from the bottom up to create huge, richly colored spikes of large, showy flowers with papery, overlapping petals. Hollyhock blossoms can be single or double and come in a wide range of colors including red, pink, yellow, tan, and maroon.

HOW TO GROW

Hollyhocks thrive in ordinary, well-drained soil and prefer the warmer spots in the garden. In ideal conditions, new shoots arise from the crown of the original plant, allowing an individual clump to produce flowers for a few more years. Self-sown plants are freely produced, ensuring hollyhock's presence in the garden. Space new plants far enough apart to ensure good air circulation. Most varieties require staking. Remove and destroy leaves diseased with hollyhock rust (yellow areas on upper leaf, orange dots underneath). Trim plants to the ground after blooming and remove all leaves and stems from the garden every fall. Pick off Japanese beetles, snails, slugs, and caterpillars by hand.

HOW TO USE

Collect flowers as they open, and snip off and discard the bitter-tasting base of the petals. Dip in light batter and fry, or brew the petals in hot water for a tea traditionally used as a remedy for indigestion or sore throat. The purple petals of *A.* 'Nigra' add smoothness and a dark tea-like color to herbal teas.

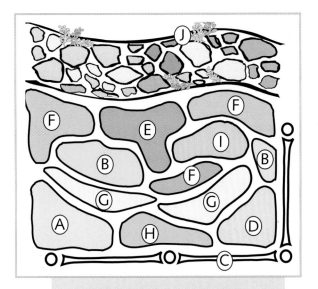

Top Choices

- *A.* 'Chater's Double' grows 8 feet tall, has fully double flowers, and comes in bright shades of pink, salmon, scarlet, and yellow.

- *A.* 'Nigra' bears single, 5- to 6-inch-wide, dark purple flowers on sturdy stems.

- *A.* 'Peaches 'n' Dreams' reaches 6 feet tall with abundant orange-peach, fully double blossoms.

- *A.* 'Summer Carnival' bears orange-bronze, double flowers on sturdy 5-foot stems.

A VICTORIAN-STYLE COTTAGE GARDEN

The hollyhock was a key element in the traditional English cottage garden, which was filled with plants and flowers useful for healing, cooking, and making potpourri. Cottage-garden plants with Old-World charm include:

- **A** *Alcea rosea* (hollyhock)
- **B** *Bellis perennis* (English daisy)
- **C** *Clematis*
- **D** *Delphinium*
- **E** *Dianthus* (pink)
- **F** *Lavandula angustifolia* (English lavender)
- **G** *Lilium* (lily)
- **H** *Rosa* (old garden roses)
- **I** *Stachys byzantina* (lamb's ears)
- **J** *Thymus* (thyme)

CHIVES
Allium schoenoprasum

Zones: 3–9

Type: Perennial

Light: Full sun or part shade

Size: 1 ft. tall, 1 ft. wide

Interest: Pink to light purple pompon-like flowers crowning a clump of narrow, hollow leaves

Uses: Culinary, decorative, medicinal

This tough, clump-forming perennial looks pretty near the front of a flower border, where you can snip leaves and flowers as needed for salads and cooking. The 10-inch-long, dark green, onion-scented leaves are hollow and add zest to many dishes. Chives belong to the same family as onions, but they produce many little bulbils from which emerge the characteristic foliage and erect flower stems. The 1-inch, globe-shaped, lavender flowers are as tasty as they are decorative.

HOW TO GROW

Chives prefer full sun and a soil that is rich, moist, and well drained, but they are more tolerant of wet, heavy soil and shade than most alliums. The plants are easy to grow and multiply quickly. To renew older clumps, divide every three to four years, keeping a cluster of at least six bulbs per division. Snipping individual leaves encourages new growth all season long. To grow a new crop of foliage, cut the leaves back to the ground after flowering.

Propagate from seeds or by division in spring or fall. Chives are free of pests and diseases. Some gardeners report that carrots and parsley taste better when grown near a clump of chives.

HOW TO USE

The flowers, bulbs, and foliage of chives lend a light onion flavor to salads and many other dishes. Add the chopped leaves to cream cheese or sour cream to make a tasty spread or dip. Use leaves and flowers as a decorative garnish for soups, stews, salads, omelettes, and baked potatoes. Freeze chopped leaves for winter use.

Garlic

- *A. sativum*, garlic, grows to 3 feet tall and 1 foot wide, with a clump of long, flat leaves and a central stem topped with white to pale pink flowers. Garlic does best in full sun and well-drained, fertile soil. Harvest garlic bulbs when the leaves turn brown in late summer to fall. Dry cloves for a few days before storing. Zones 4 to 9.

- *A. tuberosum*, garlic chives, forms a clump of narrow leaves up to 2 feet tall and 1 foot wide. It bears fragrant white flowers in late summer. Use the spicy fresh buds and leaves in salads and stir-fries. Zones 3 to 9.

CREATING A GARLIC BRAID

Braids of dried garlic make attractive kitchen decorations.

1 After harvesting the bulbs, allow the leaves to dry for a few hours until they begin to wilt.

2 Bundle five to seven bulbs together, and weave the leaves into a braid.

3 Hang the finished braid in a warm, dry place to cure.

DILL

Anethum graveolens

Zones: All

Type: Annual

Light: Full sun

Size: 3–5 ft. tall,
1 ft. wide

Interest: Fine, feathery
foliage crowned with
airy umbels of tiny yel-
low flowers that
attract bees

Uses: Culinary, decora-
tive, medicinal

Dill looks good and tastes even better. Often associat-
ed with pickles, the flavor of dill seeds is sharp and
spicy. The delicate foliage is as tasty as the seeds and is
used to season dips, breads, and other dishes. From
spring to early summer, the neat gray-green mound of
fragrant foliage adds a delicate texture to the garden. In
midsummer, the plant sends up a strong stem topped
with large yellow flower heads. With its ferny leaves,
strong scent, and large open umbels of yellow flowers,
dill adds charm to both ornamental and edible gardens.

HOW TO GROW

Dill does best in full sun and loose, fertile, well-drained
soil amended with compost. Since it does not like to be
transplanted, seeds should be sown where you want the
plants to grow. Sow in early spring in the North, in late

fall and winter in the South. Dill often self-sows. Sow once in spring if you are growing dill for its seeds, since dill planted early in the season will send up a flower stalk, or bolt, in the heat of summer. Sow at monthly intervals until midsummer to ensure a continuous harvest of leaves. Black swallowtail butterfly caterpillars feast on dill, so plant enough for you and for them. For impact and fullness, dill looks best grown in clusters of several plants each.

HOW TO USE

The cut flowers of dill add interest to summer arrangements or can be added as seasoning to vegetable recipes or baked goods. Its seeds and leaves are popular ingredients in pickles and in Indian and Scandinavian cuisines. For a scrumptious vegetable dip, mix minced dill leaves with sour cream or yogurt, or add fresh dill weed to purchased ranch or onion dip.

Top Choices

- *A.* 'Bouquet' is compact and produces abundant seed heads.

- *A.* 'Dukat' has abundant, thick foliage and is slow to flower, or bolt. *A.* 'Superdukat' has a stronger flavor than 'Dukat' with flowers of uniform height.

- *A.* 'Long Island Mammoth' produces few leaves and very large seed heads on 3-foot-tall stems.

HARVESTING
DILL SEEDS

It's easy to stock your kitchen with dill seeds from your herb garden.

1 After the seeds have started to brown, cut the seed heads from the stems. Place the seed heads upside down in a small plastic bag.

2 While holding the stems, shake the bag. The seeds will fall to the bottom of the bag. Discard the stems and store the seeds in a cool, dry place.

BENEFICIAL EFFECTS

- Dill flowers attract insects that prey on aphids.

- Plant dill near cabbage, cucumbers, and lettuce for its salutary effects as an insect repellent.

- Because dill and fennel may cross-fertilize, it is best to plant them far apart.

ANGELICA
Angelica archangelica

Zones: 4–7

Type: Biennial or short-lived perennial

Light: Part sun to light shade

Size: 3–6 ft. tall, 3 ft. wide

Interest: Tall, strong stalks with umbels of greenish white flowers

Uses: Culinary, decorative, medicinal

Bold clumps of coarse-textured, compound leaves and spheres of starry flowers make angelica a distinctive addition to any garden. It is a dramatic, sculptural plant, growing up to 6 feet tall. In its first season, the plant puts out a rosette of dark green leaves. In its second year, angelica produces strong, ribbed stalks topped with spheres of tiny greenish yellow flowers held high above the leaves.

HOW TO GROW
Angelica requires rich, moist soil in part sun to light shade. If the plants fail to bloom, the clumps can be divided to encourage flowering. Plant the divisions 3 feet apart. Angelica frequently self-sows; volunteer seedlings should be transplanted in early spring before the long taproot develops. To prolong the life of these short-lived perenni-

als, cut off the blossoms before they produce seeds. Angelica should be mulched to keep the roots moist and cool. It does not do well in areas with hot summers.

HOW TO USE

Angelica has a mild, sweet, licorice flavor. Harvest leaves from spring to summer, stems in early summer. Use the fresh leaves in salads, or cook the leaves and stems as a vegetable. The candied flower stems (see page 23) are delightful when sliced and added to desserts. This herb is also used as a natural sweetener in rhubarb dishes. The aromatic seeds are useful in perfumery, while the roots and seeds add flavor to some liqueurs.

CAUTION: *Angelica may cause skin rashes. The plant should be consumed sparingly and is not recommended during pregnancy or for those with diabetes.*

Top Choices

- *A. atropurpurea*, alexanders, has strong 6-foot-tall stems and clusters of white flowers in summer. Zones 3 to 7.

- *A. gigas*, Korean angelica, produces deep purple stems that are 4- to 5-feet-tall and topped with rounded burgundy-violet flower umbels up to 6 inches wide. Zones 5 to 9.

- *A. polymorpha* var. *sinensis*, Chinese angelica, is a tender perennial with bold, deeply divided leaves and greenish white flowers on 3-foot-tall stems. Zones 9 to 10.

Taylor's Tips

HARVESTING
ANGELICA

For best flavor, harvest angelica and other herbs early in the morning after the wet drops of dew have dried from the leaves, but before the heat of the sun diminishes the herb's essential oils.

CAUTION: Do not harvest or use angelica from the wild, because it closely resembles water hemlock, which is an extremely poisonous look-alike.

WORLDLY
ANGELICA

In addition to being a popular herb in North America, angelica is used in many places around the world. In northern Europe, the leaves are a popular vegetable. In Asia, Chinese angelica has long been regarded as one of the most potent and versatile of all herbs, second only to ginseng.

FRENCH TARRAGON
Artemisia dracunculus var. *sativa*

Zones: 3–8

Type: Perennial

Light: Full sun

Size: 2 ft. tall,
2 ft. wide

Interest: Abundant,
smooth, fragrant
foliage on upright,
branched stems

Uses: Aromatic,
culinary

Grown for its aromatic, pungent flavor, French tarragon is a favorite culinary herb. This spreading perennial has dark green, aromatic leaves. The species name, *dracunculus,* derives from tarragon's ancient reputation as a dragon herb; it was said that it would heal toxic bites and stings. The flavorless leaves of Russian tarragon, *A. dracunculus,* have no culinary value.

How to Grow
French tarragon is a vigorous plant that needs little care other than shearing the stems to the ground in spring before new growth begins. The plants thrive in full sun and well-drained soil, and need extra water only during very dry periods. Mulch roots in winter to protect them from heaving of the soil, and divide every few years to

retain vigor. French tarragon does not set seeds; propagate by division or root cutting.

HOW TO USE

An indispensable ingredient of *sauce béarnaise* and *fines herbes*, French tarragon also adds a classy touch to egg, chicken, and fish dishes as well as herbal mustards and vinegars. Harvest sprigs as needed from spring to fall to use fresh, dried, or frozen.

CAUTION: *In medicines and aromatherapy, tarragon is said to aid digestion and menstrual problems. For this reason it is not recommended for use during pregnancy.*

Other Artemesias

Consider these inedible artemesias for ornamental use only. They may be dangerous if ingested.

- *A. abrotanum*, southernwood, grows 3 feet tall and 1 to 2 feet wide with silvery green foliage and clusters of tiny yellow flowers. Use the leaves in sachets to repel moths. Zones 5 to 9.

- *A. absinthium*, wormwood, has shrubby, 2- to 3-foot-tall stems and aromatic silvery green foliage. Its leafy stems can be dried for holiday wreaths and decorations. Zones 5 to 9. 'Lambrook Silver' has especially silky silvery foliage. Zones 5 to 8.

- *A.* 'Powis Castle' forms a 3- to 4-foot mound of beautiful silvery green foliage. It is the best artemisia for the South. The leaves can be dried for use in sachets. Zones 6 to 8.

MAKING TARRAGON VINEGAR

French tarragon is a popular ingredient in herbal vinegar. Flavorful tarragon vinegar can add a delightful zing to salad dressings and vinaigrettes.

1 Pick 1 cup or more of fresh tarragon in the morning when leaves are dry.

2 Remove any damaged leaves, then bruise the remaining sprigs by rolling them between the palms of your hands. Place bruised leaves in a bottle.

3 Heat 1 pint of high-quality wine or cider vinegar and pour over the herb. Secure the lid and allow the vinegar to steep for a few days before using.

4 For a much appreciated culinary gift, remove the bruised herbs from the vinegar and add a decorative sprig of fresh tarragon to the bottle. Tie a pretty ribbon around the bottle neck for additional appeal.

5 Store in a cool, dark place.

ENGLISH DAISY
Bellis perennis

Zones: 8–10

Type: Perennial often grown as an annual or biennial

Light: Full sun or part shade

Size: 6 in. tall, 6 in. wide

Interest: Small, daisy-like flowers sitting above a rosette of dark green leaves

Uses: Culinary, decorative, medicinal

This charming little plant looks perfect along the edge of a border or path or planted among spring bulbs in a rock garden or container. Traditionally, English daisies have also been planted in lawns, where the green grass serves as a background for the tidy flowers that bloom from spring to fall. The plentiful, 1-inch blossoms have a central yellow disk surrounded by abundant, petal-shaped ray flowers. Leaves are small and obovate, arranged in a basal rosette from which the daisies rise on short, supple stems.

HOW TO GROW

Native to Europe, English daisies grow well in a wide range of conditions but prefer moist, well-drained, fertile soil in full sun to part shade. To lengthen the period of bloom, remove the spent flowers and provide some shade in midafternoon where summers are hot. Propagate by sowing seeds directly in the garden in fall for bloom the following spring, or start seeds indoors in late winter and set plants in the garden after the last frost.

HOW TO USE

Use the buds, ray flowers, and leaves of English daisy to add a sharp, fresh taste to salads, or cook the leaves for a green vegetable. The plant was a popular topical balm for joint pain and bruising in England during the sixteenth century.

Top Choices

- *B.* 'Alba Plena' is an ancient cultivar with double, white blossoms on 4-inch stems.

- *B.* 'Goliath' has very large, double blossoms up to 3 inches wide in shades of red, pink, or white on 8-inch stems.

- *B.* 'Kito' bears fully double, strawberry red flowers on 6-inch stems.

- *B.* 'Pomponette' forms a neat mound of deep green foliage topped with semi-double to double 1-inch flowers in pink, rose, or white. It is excellent for rock gardens and as an edging plant.

- *B.* 'Prolifera', with its double, white flowers tipped with pink, has been grown since the time of Shakespeare. Often, a flush of smaller flowers appears beneath the main blossom.

DIVIDING ENGLISH DAISY

In the South where the English daisy is a perennial, propagate by division.

1 Dig up the plant, bringing up enough soil to keep the root system intact as much as possible.

2 Use a clean, sharp kitchen knife to cut through the plant and its roots. Make two to four equal sections, depending on the size of the original plant. Discard any old, less vigorous roots from the center of the plant.

3 Plant the divisions about 6 inches apart.

BEAUTIFUL NAMES

The name *Bellis* derives from *bellus,* the Latin word for "beautiful," a lovely tribute to the attractiveness of this prolific, colorful flower. ✂

BORAGE
Borago officinalis

Zones: All

Type: Annual

Light: Full sun

Size: 2–3 ft. tall, 1–2 ft. wide

Interest: Open clusters of blue flowers attractive to honeybees

Uses: Culinary, decorative, medicinal

Borage has a bushy habit with dark green leaves and star-shaped, lapis blue flowers accented with black stamens. The foliage, stems, and buds are covered with silvery hairs that give the entire plant a soft metallic sheen, making the flowers even more vibrant. It is best placed toward the center of an herb border behind tidier plants. In addition to the pretty flowers, borage leaves, blossoms, and stems add a light, refreshing taste to baked dishes and summer salads.

HOW TO GROW

A native of the Mediterranean region, borage does best in full sun and well-drained soil that has been amended with some compost or rotted manure. Propagate by sowing seeds in pots and transplanting to the garden in spring, or direct-sow in early spring. Space plants 15 inches apart. Borage often self-sows if allowed to go to seed. The plants look and taste best before and during blossoming. Borage deteriorates after blooming and becomes mildew-prone in warm, humid conditions. In hot climates with long summers, repeat sowings for a continual supply of fresh, handsome plants. Once flowers have gone by, the plants should be removed from the garden. Japanese beetles may appear on the leaves in summer. Remove them by hand in the morning, when they are sluggish, and drop in a can of soapy water.

HOW TO USE

Fresh borage leaves add a delightful, subtle taste to cool summer drinks. If you don't mind the bristly texture of the fresh plant, use chopped borage leaves to add a cucumberlike flavor to garden salads. The flavorful young leaves can be cooked as a vegetable, or chopped finely and blended with cream cheese for a tasty spread. Candy the flowers or add to a variety of vegetable dishes as a garnish. Toss a handful of the blossoms over fruit salad or use to decorate frosted cakes. They also can be frozen in ice cubes for a bright addition to drinks. Borage leaves are best when used fresh, since they do not dry or freeze well.

Top Choices

- *B.* 'Alba' has deep green leaves on 3-foot-tall stems, with sprays of clear white flowers in summer.

- *B.* 'Variegata' grows 3 feet tall with blue flowers and green leaves etched with white.

MAKING CANDIED BORAGE

Candy borage flowers for a garnish by lightly painting them with egg whites and then dipping them in very fine sugar. A mixture of 1 tablespoon of gum arabic and 1 tablespoon of warm water can be substituted for the raw egg whites if desired.

THE OTHER BORAGE

Borage, *Borago officinalis,* has a close relative that is beautiful in rock gardens. Dwarf borage, *Borago pygmaea,* is more compact and slightly smaller than borage, reaching about 2 feet tall. It does not have the same culinary or medicinal value as borage, but it is more ornamental. The plants bear bright blue, nodding flowers all summer long. Try them in a rock garden, or as an accent in borders and beds of colorful annuals.

POT MARIGOLD
Calendula officinalis

Zones: All

Type: Annual

Light: Full sun

Size: Up to 2 ft. tall;
1 ft. wide

Interest: Brightly colored, daisylike flowers on long-branched stems

Uses: Culinary, decorative

The cheerful blooms of pot marigold make a bright addition to any garden. Measuring up to 3 inches across, the blossoms are either single or double and range in color from cream to yellow and gold to orange. These vigorous, bushy plants grow wider throughout the season, filling spaces left open by other flowers since gone by with sunny, summer colors.

HOW TO GROW

Pot marigold is a versatile plant that does well in full sun and a wide range of soils. Sow the large seeds directly in the garden in early spring. When the seedlings are about 4 inches high, thin to 12 inches apart. Deadhead to increase the number of blooms and prolong flowering. The plants freely self-sow if allowed to go to seed. Pot marigold does best in cool weather.

In the North, the blooms appear in summer, but in the South, this plant flowers best in the cooler seasons of spring and fall. Powdery mildew sometimes covers the leaves with a whitish powder in late summer. If this disease is a problem in your area, plant pot marigold in a breezy part of the garden, spacing the plants 14 inches apart.

HOW TO USE

Pot marigolds are excellent cut flowers, adding bright shades to summer and fall arrangements. They also dry well for everlasting bouquets. The petals can be brewed into a fine tea, eaten fresh in salads, or dried into a powder and used to impart a saffron color to foods. The petals can also be blended into skin creams to soothe skin rashes.

Top Choices

- C. 'Art Shades' has double flowers in shades of orange and cream.

- C. 'Erfurter Orangefarbige' has large, fragrant flowers packed with orange petals.

- C. Fiesta Series produces compact plants with double flowers in a range of colors from creamy yellow to orange.

- C. 'Greenheart Orange' grows to 2 feet tall with masses of large flowers. Each blossom has yellow petals edged in orange around a pale green center.

- C. 'Prolifera' is an ancient variety that bears a number of small flowers on stems rising from beneath the main blossom.

Taylor's Tips

ATTRACTING AND REPELLING BUGS

Pot marigold is subject to a variety of diseases and pests. On the other hand, it has beneficial effects in the garden, helping control the bug population.

- Plant pot marigolds and French marigolds (*Tagetes*) around tomatoes and roses to help control aphids. The plants attract hover flies, whose larvae feast on aphids.

- Pot marigold may repel asparagus beetles while adding an attractive accent to asparagus beds.

- Some herbalists claim that pot marigold planted in shrub borders or herb and flower gardens also keeps dogs away.

BEWARE THE SPOTTED CUCUMBER BEETLE

The late-summer flowers of the pot marigold make a popular meal for the spotted cucumber beetle. The insects announce their presence by chewing holes in the petals of your plants. If left unchecked, they may severely damage the flower buds. To fend off an attack, spray marigolds with insecticidal soap.

RED BUSH PEPPER
Capsicum annuum var. *annuum*

Zones: All

Type: Annual

Light: Full sun

Size: 1–3 ft. tall, 1–3 ft. wide

Interest: Bright red, green, orange, yellow, brown, or purple fruit on a shrublike plant

Uses: Culinary, decorative, medicinal

Peppers can be either hot or sweet. Both are delicious, but hot peppers have more herbal and medicinal uses. Hot peppers (cayenne and chili) belong to the Longum group, one of the five main pepper categories. Compared to sweet peppers, chili and cayenne peppers are smaller and narrower and grow on smaller plants. Dwarf varieties make charming container plants and have a loose, open habit with glossy red fruit that gleams against the dark green foliage. As decorative as they are pungent, red bush peppers enhance a landscape of flowers, herbs, fruits, and vegetables.

HOW TO GROW
Peppers are tender plants that prefer warm temperatures, full sun, and moist, fertile, well-drained soil. Grow them from seeds started indoors early in spring or buy small

starter plants to set in the ground after the last frost. Use an inexpensive black plastic mulch that warms the soil to give pepper plants a boost in cool climates. Pinch back the growing point when plants are 6 inches high to encourage branching. Stake plants when fruit begins to appear, tying the side branches as the plants grow. Water regularly and fertilize lightly. Slugs, aphids, and red spider mites can be problems. Attract slugs with small dishes of beer, where they will drown. Water plants during droughts to ward off spider mites, and plant peppers with French and pot marigolds to discourage aphids.

HOW TO USE

Use chopped, uncooked hot peppers in guacamole, or add to cheese spreads; simmer with garlic in olive oil to make a spicy dressing. Dried and powdered hot peppers are used as a seasoning in many recipes. In cool, moist climates, dry peppers indoors in a hot place with plenty of sunlight. Otherwise, dry them outdoors on a screen in the sun. Make red pepper wreaths, or *ristras,* by stringing the fresh peppers together to hang in your kitchen or by the front door for a touch of the Southwest.

Top Choices

- C. 'Ancho' or 'Poblano' bears heart-shaped fruit and thrives during long, hot summers.

- Green C. 'Jalapeño' produces 2- to 3-inch-long fruit that are especially hot tasting.

- C. 'Long Red Cayenne' bears long, tapered fruit with a spicy, pungent flavor.

Taylor's Tips

CONTROLLING THE HEAT

A classic ingredient for adding a little "fire" to recipes, many hot pepper cultivars ripen sooner, bear more fruit, and are easier to grow than sweet peppers.

CAUTION: *Rubbing your eyes after chopping fresh hot peppers or after touching their seeds may cause a painful burning sensation. Wear rubber gloves when chopping, because this burning sensation can last as long as an hour!*

- The spiciness of peppers in food can be regulated by adding them to recipes just before serving. Otherwise, the dishes can become spicier than desired.

- When preparing recipes that will be stored in the refrigerator or freezer before serving, use a pinch less pepper than usual so the spicy seasoning will not develop into an overpowering and painful experience.

- To control red bush pepper's heat, remove the seeds and the white parts in the center before using; these are hotter than the colored flesh of the pepper fruit.

CARAWAY
Carum carvi

Zones: 4–8

Type: Biennial

Light: Full sun

Size: 2 ft. tall, 1 ft. wide

Interest: Umbels of tiny white or pink flowers atop slender stems with ferny foliage

Uses: Culinary, medicinal

Caraway has been a valued cooking ingredient since Middle Eastern people began using it five thousand years ago. The seeds, those familiar, chewy little crescents in rye bread, are just one of the many useful parts of this herb. The leaves, roots, and oil also have medicinal and culinary uses. Caraway produces a bushy clump of ferny foliage its first summer. In its second year, its flower stems grow 2 feet tall and are topped with umbels of tiny white flowers. Blossoms develop into longitudinally ridged capsules that ripen in late summer. Caraway leaves are similar to those of dill or fennel.

HOW TO GROW
Caraway thrives in evenly moist, well-drained soil amended with some organic matter. Sow seeds outdoors in fall or early spring, or sow in peat pots four weeks

before the last frost. Thin the seedlings to about 8 to 12 inches apart, keeping only the strongest plants. When planting outdoors, remove the bottom of the peat pot so the taproot can grow freely. Caraway roots do not like to be disturbed, so be gentle when transplanting or avoid it altogether. Plant caraway away from fennel, which may inhibit its growth, and near peas, which it benefits. Mulch to control weeds. Seeds sown in fall produce flowering plants the next summer.

HOW TO USE

Use the fresh, young caraway leaves and roots as a vegetable. Try the leaves fresh in salads, or cooked in soups and stews. The long taproot can be gathered, cleaned, and cooked like parsnip. Slice it into thin, diagonal sections and pan-fry it in butter until tender. Or slice and use it fresh in salads. Add it cooked to sauces, soups, or stews. The seeds add a pleasing pungency to breads, goulash, pork, beef, cheese, cream sauces, desserts, and Kummel, a clear German liqueur. To avoid a bitter taste, add seeds to cooked food shortly before removing from the heat.

Top Choice

- *Trachyspermum ammi,* ajowan, is an annual and a close relative of caraway. It grows to 18 inches tall with finely divided leaves and clusters of small white summer flowers. The seeds, a favorite in Indian cuisine, ripen in late summer and have a refreshing aroma similar to thyme.

HARVESTING CARAWAY SEEDS

Caraway vigorously self-sows. For that reason, harvest the seeds before the seed capsules open.

1 Cut stems when the seed heads turn brown.

2 Tie the stems together, place upside down in a brown paper bag, and hang in a warm, dry place.

3 When dry, thresh by tapping the bag against your hand so the seeds fall to the bottom.

4 Freeze the seeds for 48 hours to kill any hitchhiking pests.

5 Screen the seeds to remove any deceased bugs. Store the seeds in a sealed jar in a cool, dark place until needed.

TAMING INDIGESTION

To make a soothing aid for indigestion, crush a tablespoonful of caraway seeds and add to a cup of warm milk. Allow to steep for about 5 minutes. Strain and drink.

ROMAN CHAMOMILE
Chamaemelum nobile

Zones: 4–8

Type: Perennial

Light: Full sun

Size: 6 in. tall,
12 in. wide

Interest: Delicate, daisylike blossoms and fine, apple-scented leaves

Uses: Decorative, medicinal

Chamomile is a low, spreading plant with aromatic, feathery foliage and abundant, daisylike flowers from summer to fall. The matlike plants make a lovely ground cover for sunny places and add a delicate touch to herb and flower borders. Because of its fragrance, chamomile works well planted in pots placed where you can easily smell the aromatic blossoms and foliage. Sitting on chamomile-covered seats or walking on chamomile lawns or chamomile-lined paths also releases the plant's pleasant, enchanting scent.

HOW TO GROW

Chamomile thrives in full sun and fertile, sandy soil amended with some organic matter. Soils high in nitrogen produce plants with fewer flowers and less fragrant foliage. Chamomile prefers cool summers and even moisture; it can tolerate short periods of drought. To propagate, sow seeds in spring or divide in fall. Space plants 6 to 12 inches apart. Remove spent flowers to encourage continued bloom and to inhibit self-sowing unless you are growing a chamomile lawn (see box at right).

HOW TO USE

Dried chamomile flowers make a soothing tea that is said to relieve indigestion, induce restful sleep, and relieve fever, insomnia, menstrual pain, and digestive problems. Dry the blossoms on a paper towel or screen. Make certain that blossoms are dry before storing them in tightly closed jars. Chamomile tea, applied as a rinse, can lighten blond hair, and may prolong the life of cut flowers when added to the water. Spraying cool chamomile tea on the leaves of phlox and other garden plants is said to control powdery mildew.

Top Choices

- C. 'Flore-Pleno' has double flowers.

- C. 'Grandiflora' has slightly larger flowers than the species.

- C. 'Treneague' is flowerless and grows only 1 inch tall, making it ideal for use in lawns and for planting between paving stones.

- *Matricaria recutita*, German chamomile, is an annual with blossoms that are sometimes considered better for tea than those of other chamomiles.

MAKING A CHAMOMILE LAWN

Chamomile lawns are usually only a few square feet in size and are best used in low-traffic areas of the yard. To establish a lawn of chamomile:

1 Prepare the soil with a rake or cultivator, loosening the top few inches of soil.

2 Plant seedlings 6 inches apart, water regularly, and weed until the lawn fills in.

3 Keep the chamomile lawn mowed to 3 to 4 inches high.

QUICK & EASY CHAMOMILE HARVEST

A chamomile rake is a useful device for harvesting chamomile blossoms or gathering seedpods. Available from many herbal supply catalogs, this handheld tool skims over the tops of the plants, catching the flowers or seedpods between the tines for easy collection.

FEVERFEW

Chrysanthemum parthenium

Zones: 5–8

Type: Perennial

Light: Full sun

Size: 1–3 ft. tall, 1–2 ft. wide

Interest: Little, daisy-like flowers and pungent, ferny foliage

Uses: Decorative, insect repellent, medicinal

Feverfew is a bushy, short-lived perennial with light green, finely cut foliage and sprays of small daisies in summer, especially where the season is cool. The leaves have a strong, pungent aroma. A native of southeastern Europe to the Caucasus, this old-fashioned plant also comes in double-flowered and gold-leaved varieties.

HOW TO GROW

Feverfew is easy to grow in full sun. It requires well-drained soil and regular watering. The plants are quite vigorous and self-sow freely, though any volunteers can be easily weeded out. To control their spread, cut the plants back after flowering. Propagate species from seeds or cuttings, or by division, setting plants 3 to 4 feet apart. If aphids become a problem, wash them from the plant with a stream of water from a hose.

HOW TO USE

Feverfew makes an excellent, long-lasting cut flower. Dried blooms are suitable for teas, potpourris, and flower arrangements. An important herb in colonial gardens, feverfew derives its name from its traditional use, lowering fevers. Other traditional medicinal uses include relief of headaches, arthritis, and rheumatism. When added to soups and stews, feverfew imparts an astringent, bitter flavor. The aromatic leaves are sometimes used as an insect repellent, although the plant can cause a skin rash in some people.

CAUTION: *Recently, the excessive internal use of feverfew has been discouraged by herbalists; the plant should not be used during pregnancy.*

Top Choices

- C. 'Aureum' is a low-growing variety, reaching 1 foot tall with gold-green leaves.

- C. 'White Bonnet' bears double, snow-white flowers on strong, 2-foot-tall stems covered with aromatic foliage.

- C. 'White Wonder' is perhaps the most attractive feverfew variety, with abundant sprays of icy white, double flowers covering the 2-foot-tall plants. The leaves are nicely aromatic. 'White Wonder' is at home in the herb garden or the perennial border.

FEVERFEW AND FRIENDS

Two close relatives of feverfew, costmary and crown daisy, are charming planted with feverfew in the herb garden.

- Costmary, or bibleleaf, *C. balsamita*, grows up to 3 feet tall and bears yellow button-shaped flowers with no rays. The common name, bibleleaf, comes from colonial days, when leaves were used for bookmarks in church hymnals. It was said that nibbling on the bitter leaves helped keep people awake during long church services.

  Costmary smells like mint but has a bitter, lemony taste when cooked or brewed. It adds pungency to soups, black and herbal teas, and ales, giving rise to its other common name, alecost.

- Crown daisy, *C. coronarium*, is an easy-to-grow, sun-loving annual that can reach up to 4 feet. Its spicy leaves and yellow flowers attract butterflies and are eaten by people in the Orient.

CILANTRO, CORIANDER

Coriandrum sativum

Zones: All

Type: Annual

Light: Full sun

Size: 1–3 ft. tall, 1 ft. wide

Interest: Aromatic leaves and clusters of white or lavender flowers

Uses: Aromatic, culinary

Cilantro is a staple of Mexican and Indian cuisines. It is also used in Chinese cooking, hence its other common name, Chinese parsley. The leaves of the plant are known as cilantro, the seeds as coriander. The small white to lavender flowers are attractive, yet the plant grows so fast and goes to seed so quickly that cilantro's ornamental effect is short-lived. The leaves at the base of the plant are lobed and soft-textured, while those on the flower stem are feathery. Grow cilantro with other kitchen herbs, where you can do repeated sowings for a continuous harvest of this pungent, strong-scented herb.

HOW TO GROW

Cilantro grows well in light, well-drained soil in full sun. Because it doesn't like to be moved, sow seeds in spring where you want the plants to grow. Thin seedlings to 4 to 6 inches apart. Foliage is best when the weather is cool. Provide some afternoon shade in hot climates to protect the leaves from drying out. Plants bolt quickly when the weather turns hot and dry, an advantage if you're growing the plant for its seeds. To maintain your cilantro supply, reseed every two to four weeks beginning in spring and continuing through summer. Planting coriander near fennel may keep the fennel from setting many seeds.

HOW TO USE

The flowers, leaves, and roots are all used to flavor soups, salsas, and other spicy dishes. Coriander seeds are tasty in sweets and liqueurs and ground into curry powder. Allow them to turn pale brown on the plant, then harvest. The flavor of dried cilantro leaves cannot compare with the dusky heat of the fresh herb, so freeze fresh leaves for later culinary use (see page 116).

Top Choices

- C. 'Slo Bolt' is more heat-tolerant than the species. It produces a multitude of leaves without producing the flower stems that make the foliage bitter.

- C. 'Long Standing' is similar to other slow-bolting varieties with dark green, ferny leaves.

- C. 'Santo' is another variety that is slow to flower, producing abundant crops of tasty, deep green leaves.

Taylor's Tips

USING CORIANDER SEED

Harvest your own coriander seeds, or buy them at the market for grinding. They are also available in powder form. To harvest, simply place the flower heads in a paper bag, then grasp the stems with the bag and shake to loosen the seeds. Store in a cool, dry place and grind with a mortar and pestle when ready to use.

CILANTRO OR CORIANDER?

Cilantro and coriander are not different plants, just names for different parts of the same plant. The leaves and stems of *Coriandrum sativum* are called cilantro, the familiar green stuff in salsa. The seeds, which have a sharp but sweet orange taste, are called coriander.

CLOVE PINK
Dianthus caryophyllus

Zones: 8–10

Type: Perennial often grown as an annual

Light: Full sun

Size: 1–2 ft. tall, less than 1 ft. wide

Interest: Pretty pink to purple flowers against glaucous blue-green leaves

Uses: Aromatic, culinary, decorative

Clove pink has dainty, fringed, deep pink blossoms that glow against mounds of silvery blue-green stems and narrow foliage. What stands out most about this plant, in addition to its charming appearance, is its spicy fragrance. Although this species includes the large-bloomed florists' carnations, these have no fragrance. Other scented pinks include the cottage pinks, *D.* x *allwoodii*, which are hardy to Zone 4 and bloom for as long as two months. As their name implies, they look lovely in a cottage garden.

HOW TO GROW

Clove pink thrives in rich, well-drained soil with a neutral to slightly alkaline pH. It benefits from being cut back after blooming. The roots prefer to be evenly moist, while the foliage and flowers do best in warm, dry conditions. In humid locations, clove pink can suffer viral and fungal diseases that weaken the plants, opening the way for infestations of aphids, thrips, and spider mites. To propagate, start seeds indoors in late winter or divide established plants in late summer.

HOW TO USE

Cut flowers in midmorning for bouquets, or dry them for use in potpourri. The raw petals, minus the bitter white base, add a delightful, floral flavor to salads. Use the petals as an ingredient in herbal butter, or candy them (see page 23) to decorate desserts. The petals add a spicy flavor to wines and vinegar, and make a sweet syrup when boiled with sugar and water.

Other Dianthus

- *D.* x *allwoodii* 'Alpinus', cottage pink, is a very hardy strain that forms a tidy mound of bluish gray foliage sprinkled with fragrant, single flowers from spring to summer. Zones 3 to 7.

- *D. barbartus,* sweet William, is a biennial or short-lived perennial with slender, dark green leaves and clusters of colorful flowers atop 1- to 2-foot-tall stems in late spring to early summer. Zones 3 to 10.

- *D. chinensis,* China pink, is an easy-to-grow annual with clusters of usually scentless flowers on 18-inch stems.

A SHORT COURSE ON SOIL pH

Testing your soil is one way to make sure that you are providing the best growing conditions for your plants to thrive.

Clove pink prefers neutral to slightly alkaline soil to grow best. You can test the relative acidity or alkalinity of your soil with a soil-testing kit, available from most nurseries and garden centers.

Neutral pH is 7. Any number below that is acidic; above is alkaline. Most plants do well in slightly acidic to neutral soil with a pH of 6 to 7.

To render soil more alkaline, add lime to it according to the results of the soil test. Soil in the hot, dry climate of the Southwest tends to be alkaline, while soil in forested areas of the Northeast and Northwest is often acidic.

PURPLE CONEFLOWER
Echinacea purpurea

Zones: 4–8

Type: Perennial

Light: Full sun

Size: 3–4 ft. tall, 2 ft. wide

Interest: Drooping, rosy purple ray flowers around a dark bronze central cone

Uses: Decorative, medicinal

The spiky, pointed, orange disk of the purple coneflower gives this stately herb its other name, hedgehog coneflower. Its rough, dark green foliage contrasts handsomely with its 3- to 4-inch, daisylike blooms that range in color from icy white to burgundy, depending on the cultivar. Purple coneflower's strong, erect habit, coarse foliage, and majestic blossoms lend a bold presence when massed in the border or planted in rows in a cutting garden. This native herb provides a nectar source in butterfly gardens and wildflower meadows.

HOW TO GROW

Purple coneflower is a rugged plant that thrives in a range of soils, and is heat- and drought-tolerant. Do not fertilize, because the plants may become floppy and require staking. Propagate by dividing clumps in spring or fall. Space plants 18 to 24 inches apart to promote good air circulation, which inhibits the growth of mildew on the leaves. Old, thick clumps can be thinned by division or selective pruning. If Japanese beetles are a problem, pick them off by hand and drop them in a jar of soapy water.

HOW TO USE

Purple coneflower makes an excellent, long-lasting cut flower. Its seed heads look equally striking in fresh or dry arrangements. This native herb, which still grows wild in the prairies and fields of the central United States, was used for centuries as a medicine by native North Americans, particularly the Plains Indians. The dried roots are used to stimulate the immune system and can help reduce the severity of cold and flu symptoms. The roots are lifted and dried in fall to make medicinal powders, tinctures, and infusions.

CAUTION: *People with immune-system disorders such as diabetes or AIDS must check with their doctors before using purple coneflower.*

Top Choices

- *E.* 'Bright Star' is 2 to 3 feet tall with rosy pink petals and a maroon cone.

- *E.* 'Magnus' has large rose-purple flowers on strong, 3-foot-tall stems.

- *E.* 'White Swan' has pure white ray flowers and grows 18 to 24 inches tall.

GATHERING ROOTS WHILE GROWING FLOWERS

Purple coneflower is one of the most beautiful plants in the herb garden, yet its most potent medicinal part is not the flower but the root. The roots of purple coneflower can be collected without harvesting the entire plant.

1 To have both medicinal roots and beautiful flowers, allow plants to grow undisturbed until they form a thick clump, about three to four years.

2 In spring or fall, lift the clump from the ground with a garden fork and shake off excess soil.

3 Divide the clump with a sharp knife, leaving each division with plenty of roots.

4 Cut the longest root from each division and set aside so that the remaining roots are left intact. Replant the division in the desired location.

5 Wash the taproot; place in a warm, dark room until completely dry. Store in a dark-colored glass jar that is tightly sealed.

FENNEL
Foeniculum vulgare

Zones: 6–9

Type: Biennial or perennial grown as an annual

Light: Full sun

Size: Up to 6 ft. tall, 2 ft. wide

Interest: Large, flat, yellow flower heads and fragrant, needle-thin foliage

Uses: Aromatic, culinary, decorative

Fennel stands tall in the garden, with its threadlike, shiny leaves and hollow stems towering over many other kitchen herbs. The broad umbels of flat, yellow, summer flowers give way to sweet, anise-flavored, brown seeds in fall. Attractive though fennel is, consider carefully where you grow it, since its presence may have a detrimental effect on the size and viability of other garden plants, including many vegetables and herbs.

HOW TO GROW
Fennel prefers full sun and well-drained, alkaline soil amended with organic matter. Propagate from seeds sown in early spring or fall. In warmer areas where fennel is a perennial, divide in spring. Deadhead flowers to keep plants from self-sowing. Grow fennel as far away from coriander as possible, since this herb is reported to

inhibit seed formation in fennel. Although fennel will not harm dill, keep these plants apart because of their tendency to cross-fertilize.

HOW TO USE

Fennel is an herb with many uses. The anise-scented yellow flowers are long-lasting additions to fresh flower arrangements. The seeds and leaves make an excellent herb tea and add a flavorful accent to soups, stews, and stuffings. In addition, the seeds can be chewed as a breath sweetener and were eaten on fast days to curb hunger pangs. Herbalists believed fennel relieved flatulence, increased the supply of mother's milk, encouraged weight loss, and acted as an aphrodisiac.

Top Choices

- *F.* 'Purpurascens', bronze fennel, is a 5-foot-tall, ornamental variety with lacy purple-bronze foliage that enhances the appearance of many closely situated garden flowers.

- *F.* 'Smokey' has lacy bronze-colored foliage with a delicate licorice flavor. This variety matures about ten days earlier than many other varieties.

- *F. vulgare* var. *azoricum*, Florence fennel, grows to 2 feet tall. Its bulbous base is often eaten as a vegetable, cooked or raw. Zones 5 to 9.

Taylor's Tips

COOKING WITH FENNEL

The delicate flavor of fennel leaves is rapidly diminished by cooking. When using fresh leaves in cooked dishes, add them a minute or two before serving to ensure the best flavor retention. The seeds are less heat-sensitive; add to recipes at any time during the preparation period. The bulb-like base of Florence fennel can be cooked and served with melted butter.

Bronze fennel has the same flavor as fennel but is more decorative, adding a little panache to the garden.

SWEET WOODRUFF
Galium odoratum

Zones: 4–8

Type: Perennial

Light: Full to part shade

Size: 1 ft.-tall ground cover

Interest: Fragrant, starry, white flowers on a spreading mat of whorled, rich green leaves

Uses: Aromatic, decorative

In late spring, sweet woodruff bears loose clusters of tiny, four-petaled, vanilla-scented flowers on slender stems. In winter, the abundant green leaves turn tan, adding subtle interest to the landscape. The species name, *odoratum*, means "fragrant." The flowers and foliage have the scent of vanilla when cut or dried.

HOW TO GROW

Sweet woodruff prefers a shady location in the South, where it is evergreen in winter and may die back in summer. In the North, it requires at least part shade; the deep green summer foliage dies and dries to a warm tan in winter. A woodland species, sweet woodruff thrives in moist, rich, acidic soil beneath the canopies of deciduous trees. It even grows well near pines and hemlocks, where most other plants falter. The plant spreads easily, especially when adequate moisture is provided. Virtually carefree, sweet woodruff makes an excellent ground cover. The seeds are difficult to germinate; instead, set out starter plants in spring or fall. Propagate by division in spring or fall.

HOW TO USE

Unlike many other herbs, which are most aromatic when fresh, the leaves of sweet woodruff become increasingly fragrant as they dry. An ingredient in Alsatian May wine, sweet woodruff can also be mixed with other fragrant plants in potpourri (although its crumbly nature may make the potpourri look a little dusty). The aromatic dried leaves were strewn onto floors to sweeten the air in medieval dwellings.

Lady's Bedstraw

- *G. verum*, yellow bedstraw, is a hardy, spreading perennial that grows up to 3 feet high with abundant clusters of tiny, sunny yellow, sweet-smelling flowers in summer. Long ago, it was used with other herbs as a mattress stuffing. Take care when planting, because it is quite invasive, having established itself as a roadside weed in the northeastern United States. It's a good choice for sunny meadow gardens. Zones 3 to 8.

Taylor's Tips

CONTROLLING SWEET WOODRUFF

At first glance, sweet woodruff looks like a fragile little plant, but it is remarkably tough and vigorous. Once established, it spreads quickly and can invade space reserved for other plants.

It's easy to keep this delicate, beautiful ground cover in bounds and gather all the sweet woodruff you need at the same time. Simply pull up shoots that appear in undesirable places.

If this is done in late summer, the collected stems and leaves are most abundant. They can then be dried for stuffing herbal pillows or sachets. (Because dried sweet woodruff crumbles easily, it is not the best candidate for long-lasting herbal wreaths.)

SUNFLOWER
Helianthus annuus

Zones: All

Type: Annual

Light: Full sun

Size: Up to 10 ft. tall, 1–2 ft. wide

Interest: Very large, drooping flower heads with yellow ray flowers and dark centers on tall, thick stalks

Uses: Culinary, decorative

Sunflowers are perky, vigorous plants that add architectural interest to the garden and attract birds and butterflies. Revered by the ancient Incas in Peru and cultivated by Native Americans for more than three thousand years, this native plant is still beloved by children and adults alike. On sunny days the large flower heads follow the sun across the sky. Sunflower seeds are easy to plant, germinate quickly, and grow fast, making this plant a favorite for children's gardens. The cheerful yellow blossoms give way to seed-filled flower heads that become hubs of activity for hungry birds, squirrels, and people.

HOW TO GROW
Sunflowers like well-drained soil in full sun. Sow seeds in the garden about ½ inch deep in spring after the last

frost. Thin seedlings to stand 12 inches apart. Keep well watered and mulch around the base of the plants to keep the soil cool.

HOW TO USE

The small-flowered types of sunflower look terrific in bouquets. The seeds of the mammoth varieties can be ground into meal, Native American style, or eaten raw or toasted, as a snack. The seeds lend a nutty taste to baked products, and their oil is used for cooking and salad dressings. Consuming sunflower seeds is said to help lower blood cholesterol levels.

Top Choices

- *H.* 'Elf', a dwarf cultivar, has 4-inch-wide flowers on an 18-inch-tall plant.

- *H.* 'Giant Grey Stripe' grows up to 15 feet tall with a seed head up to 15 inches wide.

- *H.* 'Sunrich Lemon' is a hybrid that bears a large, clear yellow flower head, stands 4 feet tall, and is pollen-free, making it perfect for cutting gardens.

- *H.* 'Teddy Bear' bears double, yellow flowers on bushy plants 2 feet tall.

- *H. tuberosus*, Jerusalem artichoke, grows 8 feet tall with small yellow blooms like little sunflowers. It has edible, sweet, nutty tubers, considered a delicacy by some.

ATTRACTING BIRDS TO THE GARDEN

Sunflowers produce abundant supplies of food for many species of birds. The tall, large-flowered varieties, such as 'Giant Grey Stripe', yield the most seeds. Surround tall types with clumps of small-blossomed forms. Some of the birds that are especially attracted to sunflowers include:

- ~ blackbirds
- ~ cardinals
- ~ chickadees
- ~ crossbills
- ~ goldfinches
- ~ grackles
- ~ grosbeaks
- ~ jays
- ~ nuthatches
- ~ purple finches
- ~ slate-colored juncos
- ~ sparrows
- ~ titmice
- ~ towhees

CURRY PLANT
Helichrysum angustifolium

Zones: 9–10

Type: Perennial grown as an annual

Light: Full sun

Size: 2 ft. tall, 2 ft. wide

Interest: Dark yellow, everlasting flowers on a silvery, fragrant, bushy plant

Uses: Aromatic, decorative, medicinal

During the summer months, curry plant looks like a small silver bush with its pewter gray, needlelike foliage and 2-inch terminal clusters of dark yellow flower heads. During the colder months, the everlasting blossoms add summer beauty to dried arrangements. The plant looks wonderful in a pot on the patio, where you can appreciate its appearance and fragrance close up. Curry plant derives its common name from its aromatic leaves, which smell like Indian curry powder. It is not, however, the source of curry powder, which is a blend of several spices.

HOW TO GROW
A native of the Mediterranean region, curry plant grows best in raised beds or in full sun and loose, well-drained, sandy soil. In areas where they are perennial, the plants

are susceptible to root rot during moist winters. Although regular watering stimulates growth, the plant can tolerate periods of dry weather. Prune back the side stems to encourage branching. Aphids and mealybugs may be a problem, especially during periods of warm, humid weather. Propagate from cuttings in spring or late summer.

HOW TO USE

Cut and dry everlasting flowers for use in dried arrangements. Harvest tender young leaves from spring to fall to use fresh in salads or add to cooked dishes for a light curry taste.

Top Choices

- *H.* 'Nana' is a dwarf variety with bright yellow flowers and aromatic leaves. Zones 9 to 10.

- *H. bracteatum,* strawflower, bears pink, red, orange, cream, or gold everlasting blooms on strong stems up to 30 inches tall. Strawflowers are excellent for cutting and drying for decorative arrangements.

- *H.* 'Bright Bikini' reaches 15 inches tall with everlasting blooms in a wide range of colors.

- *H.* 'Silvery Rose' reaches 30 inches tall with large, pink, double flowers brushed with rose.

- *H. petiolare* 'Limelight' has felt-like, pale green leaves. Zones 8 to 10.

HARVESTING EVERLASTINGS

Harvest everlastings such as curry plant before the flowers open completely.

1 Cut flowering stems in the late morning, keeping them as long as possible.

2 Hang the stems upside down in bunches in a warm, dry space with adequate air circulation (such as an attic) for one to two months.

3 Use alone or as a filler in dried floral arrangements.

DAYLILY
Hemerocallis

Zones: 4–9

Type: Perennial

Light: Full sun to part shade

Size: 10–60 in. tall, up to 30 in. wide; blossoms 2–9 in. across

Interest: Colorful blooms rise above a mound of elegant, straplike foliage

Uses: Culinary, decorative

Daylilies are among the most elegant of plants, easy to grow, and wonderfully tasty. Blossom shapes range from the classic trumpet to a delicate spidery form. The season of bloom varies with the species or cultivar, from March in the South to August and September in the North. Some hybrids, such as 'Stella de Oro', 'Black-Eyed Stella', and lemony 'Happy Returns', bloom all summer long. Daylily habits also vary from circular mounds to spreading ground covers. The plants look great in tubs, in massed plantings, or in mixed borders. Colors vary but the tastiest varieties are yellow.

HOW TO GROW
Daylilies thrive in full sun but also do very well in part shade. They like loose, well-drained, fertile soil. Water regularly for maximum growth. Spacing holes 1 to 2 feet

apart, dig a hole 2 feet wide and 1 foot deep for each plant. Mix a shovelful of compost, humus, or aged manure into the removed soil and use to backfill. Mulch around the plants to maintain moisture content and encourage growth.

Evergreen varieties generally perform better in the South, while dormant kinds do best in the North. Divide daylilies when plants become crowded or when the flowers grow sparse. Daylilies are mostly pest- and disease-free and are easily propagated by division in spring or fall. However, one of the best things about daylilies is that they can grow forever without requiring division.

HOW TO USE

Daylily buds, flowers, inner leaves, and crisp root tubers can be boiled, sautéed, or stir-fried, or chopped raw for salads. Flowers, without pistil and stamens, make edible garnishes. The buds contain significant amounts of protein and vitamins A and C and are a popular ingredient in Oriental cuisine. The flowers are edible until the day after bloom; used any later, they taste bitter. The stronger the fragrance, the more flavorful the flower.

Top Choices

- Fragrant daylilies include *H.* 'Hyperion', an old-fashioned hybrid with 40-inch stalks. Fragrant yellow blooms are quite tasty.

- *H. lilioasphodelus,* lemon daylily, is an early-blooming, old-fashioned favorite with light yellow flowers on 2- to 3-foot-tall stalks. The scent is similar to honeysuckle.

DIVIDING DAYLILIES

Daylilies are vigorous, clump-forming plants. As the clump grows larger year after year, the plants near the center become overcrowded. The plants then begin to lose vitality, becoming less vigorous and producing fewer flowers. Dividing daylily clumps every three or four years is an easy way to keep the plants healthy. To divide daylilies:

1 Dig up the plant, leaving as much of the root structure intact as possible.

2 Uncover growing points by removing dirt by hand or washing the root mass with water.

3 If the roots are too tangled to separate by hand and too tough for a knife to cut, divide with a sharp spade or pull apart with two garden forks set back to back.

4 Plant the divisions and water well to settle the soil around the roots. Then add a layer of mulch to hold moisture in the soil and to keep the plant roots cool.

HYSSOP

Hyssopus officinalis

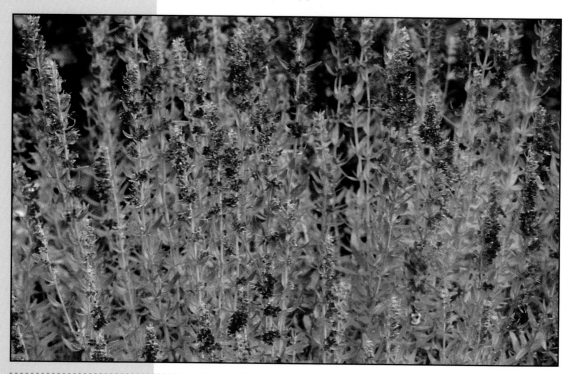

Zones: 3–9

Type: Perennial

Light: Full sun

Size: 2 ft. tall,
2 ft. wide

Interest: Blue, pink, or
white flower spikes
that attract bees and
butterflies

Uses: Aromatic, culi-
nary, decorative,
medicinal

Hyssop has two distinct and lovely garden personali-
ties. It makes a low, boxy, semi-evergreen hedge
suitable for knot gardens or formal edging, with plants
spaced 12 to 15 inches apart and sheared. Spaced 2 feet
apart and allowed to grow freely, hyssop has a relaxed,
shrubby habit and bears spikes of blue or, rarely, white
or pink flowers that grow in whorls from the leaf axils.
Hyssop is woody at the base, and its stems are covered
with shiny, narrow, dark green leaves that release a powerful musky-mint aroma when touched. In biblical times
it was considered one of the purifying herbs.

HOW TO GROW

This pest-free Mediterranean native grows well in dry,
sandy, slightly acidic to alkaline soil in full sun. Spring is
the best time to clip hyssop into hedges. Propagate from

softwood cuttings in summer, or from seeds or by root division in spring and fall. Hyssop is a slow-growing plant, so start seeds indoors for spring cultivation. Cut the plants to the ground in spring, or in mild climates, after blooming.

HOW TO USE

Hyssop flowers are useful for fresh arrangements. Harvest the tops of the stems, including flowers, when they begin to bloom. When growing hyssop for tea, cut stems to the ground before flowering and dry the leaves whole. After flowering, this plant becomes increasingly woody and loses some of its aroma. Used sparingly, hyssop flowers, stems, and leaves add zest to soups, meats, vegetables, salads, and fruit pies. Hyssop is also an ingredient in perfumes and liqueurs, especially Chartreuse.

CAUTION: *Traditionally, hyssop aids digestion and repels insects, but it is not recommended for use during pregnancy.*

Top Choices

- *H.* 'Alba' bears spikes of lovely, pure white flowers.

- *H.* 'Grandiflora' bears large lavender flowers.

- *H.* 'Roseum' produces deep rose flowers.

- *H.* 'Rosea' has lilac-pink flowers.

- *H.* 'Sissinghurst' is a dwarf form, reaching about 1 foot tall.

Taylor's Tips

LOVE IT OR HATE IT

Some plants naturally benefit others. For example, plant grapes near hyssop and the vines thrive, yielding more grapes. Cabbages love hyssop, too, because it lures away the cabbage butterfly. On the other hand, radishes do not do well planted near hyssop.

The same love-hate relationship exists in the insect world. Bees are very fond of the hyssop flowers, while most other insects are repelled by them.

MAKING HYSSOP TEA

Hyssop makes a soothing tea that is said to regulate blood pressure and relieve rheumatism.

To make hyssop tea, steep 1 teaspoon dried flower tops or leaves in 1 cup boiling water for 10 minutes. Strain and sweeten as desired.

ELECAMPANE
Inula helenium

Zones: 4–9

Type: Perennial

Light: Full sun

Size: 4–6 ft. tall, 3 ft. wide

Interest: Fine-rayed yellow daisies atop tall, large-leafed, hairy stalks

Uses: Aromatic, culinary, decorative, medicinal

This impressive plant's botanical and common name, elecampane, refers to the mythological beauty, Helen; she held a bunch of these fringed yellow flowers when she eloped with Paris to Troy. The genus name, *Inula*, is said to come from the Greek word for Helen. Elecampane is an excellent back-of-the-border or meadow plant, with 6-foot-tall stems and 16-inch, oval, pointed leaves on petioles up to 1 foot long. Farther up the sturdy stalk, the leaves grow smaller and clasp the stem. Beautiful blossoms with slender golden petals appear singly or in groups of two or three.

HOW TO GROW

Elecampane likes full sun and moist (but not wet) soil amended with organic matter. Fertilize with a 1-inch layer of composted cow manure around each plant in spring. The strikingly tall stalks are quite sturdy and do not require staking. Cut stalks to the ground after flowering.

Propagate elecampane from seeds in the spring or by root division in spring in Zones 4 to 6, and fall from Zones 7 to 9. Sow seeds directly in the garden in spring when soil is still cool and cover lightly with soil or vermiculite. Thin seedlings to stand 2 to 3 feet apart. To divide, dig up a root, slicing it into sections containing at least one bud each. Plant the segments in their new locations, leaving plenty of room for each plant to mature. Water regularly until the new shoots emerge from the soil.

HOW TO USE

Elecampane's slender yellow petals can be gathered and dried to add a cheerful touch to potpourri. The seed heads can be collected in late summer, dried, and added to winter arrangements. The sliced, candied roots have an aroma like tropical fruit and are often used to distinctively flavor desserts and liqueurs.

Also known as scabwort and horseheal, elecampane was brought to America by settlers to heal sheep scabs and horse indispositions.

Top Choices

- *I. ensifolia*, swordleaf inula, is an ornamental perennial with abundant, sunny yellow, daisylike flowers on 12-inch stems. Zones 5 to 9.

- *I.* 'Compacta' is a dwarf form that reaches about 6 inches tall and bears yellow flowers in late summer.

Taylor's Tips

CONSERVING MOISTURE

If you live in a hot, dry climate or cannot water your elecampane with any regularity, plant it in light shade and add mulch around the base of the plant to conserve moisture. Installing a soaker hose beneath the mulch is a good way to provide needed water with minimal waste.

ELECAMPANE PAST AND FUTURE

Elecampane was a popular medicinal herb in Rome, where it was used as a remedy for indigestion. Centuries later, in medieval Europe, the plant was a primary ingredient in an herbal concoction called St. Paul's wine, which was also used to relieve stomach distress. Modern researchers have determined that the herb contains chemicals with antispasmodic qualities, and may contain others with antibiotic abilities.

SWEET BAY
Laurus nobilis

Zones: 8–10

Type: Perennial shrub

Light: Full sun to part shade

Size: Up to 30 ft. tall, 25 ft. wide

Interest: Stiff, glossy, dark green leaves on a handsome shrub or medium-sized tree

Uses: Aromatic, culinary, decorative

Aromatic sweet bay leaves grow on evergreen plants that can rise as tall as 30 feet. Allowed to grow freely, their natural habit is upright and boldly attractive, with handsome leaves that are smooth, dark green, and shiny, with a prominent light midvein. Small, light yellow flowers appear in the leaf axils in spring, followed by black berries later in the growing season. Because its roots tolerate confinement, sweet bay also makes an excellent potted plant or topiary. In ancient Greece, sweet bay, also known as laurel, crowned the brows of poets and heroes, making it a truly noble herb.

HOW TO GROW
Native to the Mediterranean region, sweet bay prefers well-drained, average soil and consistent moisture. Once established, it can tolerate some dryness but requires

protection from cold winds and icy weather. In northern areas, grow bay in a container so that you can bring it indoors before the first frost. For container plants, use a potting mix that is about one-half potting soil, one-quarter peat moss, and one-quarter screened garden soil. Fertilize in late winter or spring, as new growth begins, and again in late summer. Sweet bay is not easy to propagate; try using stem cuttings taken in fall. Expect to wait six to nine months for roots to develop.

HOW TO USE

Leafy twigs of laurel add texture and fragrance to herbal wreaths and dried arrangements. The essential oil in bay leaves enhances the flavor of soups, stews, and sauces, both alone and as an ingredient in a *bouquet garni*. The aroma of bay grows more potent when dried and crushed or powdered. Bay leaves are spicier dried than fresh, and remain flavorful for about one year.

A tea made from dried or fresh bay leaves has traditionally been used to increase the appetite and aid digestion.

Top Choices

- *L.* 'Angustifolia', willow leaf bay, has slender, wavy-edged leaves.

- *L.* 'Aurea' bears golden yellow leaves that mature to pale yellow-green.

- *L.* 'Crispa' has dark green leaves with wavy margins.

Taylor's Tips

SCULPTING SWEET BAY

Sweet bay is a dense evergreen plant that is often pruned and sculpted into creative forms. Shape your bay tree in summer after the first flush of growth in spring is over. Snip the branches one by one with a sharp hand pruner, being careful not to remove more than one-half of the new growth. Do not use hedge shears, because their broad cuts can destroy the beauty of bay's lustrous green leaves.

KEEP BUGS AT BAY

Over the years, sweet bay has been used in the kitchen in many ways. One of the more unusual uses reached its peak of popularity around the turn of the century. Then people would add a few dried bay leaves to their flour bins. The oils in the leaves supposedly repelled flour moths. Try this to repel other pantry insects.

ENGLISH LAVENDER
Lavandula angustifolia

Zones: 5–9

Type: Perennial

Light: Full sun

Size: 2–3 ft. tall, 3 ft. wide

Interest: Clumps of perfumed, silvery green foliage and bright blue-purple flowering spikes

Uses: Aromatic, culinary, decorative

The distinctive aroma of lavender—familiar from soaps and perfumes—recalls the clean, sweet freshness of a warm summer morning. Planted as a low hedge or as a bushy edging along paths or walkways, lavender releases its pleasant fragrance when brushed. Massed in a perennial or mixed border, it blends with other plants and softens the strong aspect of bold colors. This Mediterranean native is drought-tolerant and grows well on dry, sunny slopes.

HOW TO GROW

This pest-free plant thrives in full sun and likes well-drained, slightly acidic to slightly alkaline, sandy soil. In mild climates, lavender becomes a woody, bushy evergreen that can be pruned at any time of year. In cold climates, however, the plant needs to be pruned to about 6 inches high or cut back near the ground if it becomes woody and unkempt. To keep lavender disease-free, provide full sun and good air circulation. To avoid root rot in heavy soil, plant lavender in raised beds so that water will not collect. Propagate by layering, by division or from cuttings in summer.

HOW TO USE

Harvest lavender flowers as they begin to open, when their fragrance is most intense. Lavender is a wonderful, long-lasting cut flower. Dried, it adds fragrance to potpourris and sachets. A small, lavender-filled muslin pillow may relieve sleeplessness and soothe the jitters. The oil of *L. angustifolia,* the most fragrant lavender, is a common ingredient in soaps and perfumes. The fresh flowers also add a unique flavor to desserts, baked goods, vinegars, and jellies.

Top Choices

- *L.* 'Hidcote' is compact and erect with deep purple flowers.
- *L.* 'Miss Katherine' has fragrant, clear pink blossoms.
- *L.* 'Munstead' has a compact habit and lavender-blue flower spikes.
- *L.* 'Lavender Lady' grows to 10 inches and flowers the first year from seeds.

PROPAGATION BY LAYERING

Use this simple layering technique for propagating lavender and other woody herbs, such as rosemary and winter savory.

1 Strip the leaves from a flexible shoot but leave the foliage on the stem tip.

2 Nick the stem where you want the roots to grow.

3 Make a shallow trench and bend the stem to the ground. Peg it into the soil, using a hairpin-shaped wire, a rock, or a small mound of soil.

4 Water regularly. After the stem has developed its own root system, sever it from its parent and replant.

LOVAGE
Levisticum officinale

Zones: 3–8

Type: Perennial

Light: Full sun to part shade

Size: Up to 6 ft. tall, about 4 ft. wide

Interest: Yellow-green flower clusters rise above a leafy, hollow-stemmed plant that smells like celery

Uses: Aromatic, culinary, medicinal, decorative

Lovage is a bold plant that looks striking at the back of the border. In summer, shiny, yellow-green, triple-compound leaves drape a scaffold of strong stems that support decorative clusters of tiny yellow flowers. The entire plant, including flowers, seeds, stems, leaves, and roots, is edible; it tastes like celery but is much easier to grow. Lovage is sometimes called loveache, in reference to its use as an aphrodisiac during the Middle Ages. Its reputation as a love potion comes not, however, from its powers but rather from the mispronunciation of *liguria*, its common name in Roman times.

HOW TO GROW
Lovage prefers a sunny to partly shady location in rich, moist soil amended with some organic matter. If you're growing lovage for its leaves and want a fuller look,

remove the flower heads before they bloom. After flowering, the celery-scented leaves may turn yellow and become tasteless, so give your plant sufficient nutrients through compost and organic fertilizers to ensure good health. Lovage needs little attention once established, but it is susceptible to leaf miners, which can be handled by removing the affected foliage. Divide in spring or plant seeds outdoors in autumn.

HOW TO USE

Harvest lovage leaves as needed in summer to add a celerylike, although much stronger, flavor to recipes. Used sparingly to avoid overwhelming the flavor of the food, lovage leaves enhance stuffings, soups, stews, mixed vegetables, and sauces. Add the seeds to baked goods and salad dressings. Harvest the stems in spring to use fresh in salads or cooked as a vegetable. Or chop and candy the stems to add to desserts (see page 23).

Traditionally, lovage was used more for medicine than food. The roots were thought to ease menstrual pain, flatulence, and kidney and digestive problems. Because of its diuretic properties, some herbalists used it to treat obesity.

Top Choice

• *Ligusticum scoticum,* Scots lovage, has dark green leaves and greenish white summer flowers on stout 2- to 3-foot-tall plants. Closely related to *Levisticum officinale,* Scots lovage is grown for its stems, which have a flavor similar to celery. Zones 5 to 8.

DRYING LOVAGE STEMS AND LEAVES

Lovage leaves and stems can be dried successfully for your favorite culinary use.

1 Choose fresh, young stalks with leaves attached. Place upside down in a brown paper bag punched with ventilation holes and hang them in a dark, warm place with good air circulation. Dry thoroughly.

2 To keep dried lovage from discoloring, store it in a sealed container away from the light.

3 Throw out unused lovage after one year.

COLLECTING LOVAGE SEEDS

Collect lovage seeds when the 1/4-inch, ridged fruit begins to open and release its seeds. Cut the stem of the seed head and hang it upside down in a paper bag. When dry, grasp the stem of the seed head together with the bag and shake to release the paired seeds. Store the seeds in a cool, dry place until ready to use in baked goods and salad dressings.

GERMAN CHAMOMILE
Matricaria recutita

Zones: All

Type: Annual

Light: Full sun

Size: 2–2½ ft. tall

Interest: A fragrant, finely textured plant with yellow-centered, daisylike flowers.

Uses: Aromatic, decorative, medicinal

Although charming and delicate in appearance, German chamomile is hardy and easy to grow—so easy, in fact, that this European and Asian native has naturalized itself in the fields and roadsides of North America. Unlike its low-growing perennial counterpart, Roman chamomile, *Chamaemelum nobile*, German chamomile is unsuitable for a lawn substitute but well adapted for the ornamental herb garden. Its applelike fragrance, feathery foliage, and 1-inch white and yellow flowers contrast nicely with coarser plants such as mint, sage, and parsley. While one plant may go unnoticed in the garden, however, several massed together have a definite, if dainty, presence. For cottage-garden appeal, let random, self-sown chamomile seedlings interweave themselves among other flowering plants.

HOW TO GROW

This easy-to-grow herb flourishes in ordinary to sandy, well-drained soil in full sun. Plants will keep blooming if you harvest blossoms as they open; otherwise, expect them to decline soon after flowering. To propagate German chamomile, sow seeds 6 inches apart in early spring or fall. To take advantage of German chamomile's tendency to self-sow, refrain from harvesting one or more plants and allow them to go to seed.

HOW TO USE

Although German chamomile is less fragrant than Roman chamomile, it contains slightly more volatile oil, so many herbalists prefer it. Dried chamomile adds a light apple aroma to herbal wreaths and potpourris. It has a relaxing effect when placed in a muslin bag and steeped in warm bathwater. Tea made from chamomile flowers may calm the nerves, soothe insomnia, and relieve indigestion and teething pain. Strong chamomile tea enhances blonde highlights when used as a hair rinse. To dry chamomile, harvest the blossoms when they open. Spread on screens to dry in a warm, airy room.

Top Choices

- *M. recutita* 'Bodegold' is a 2-foot-tall culti-var that blooms two weeks earlier than the species. Its plentiful blooms and fairly uni-form growth habit promote easy harvesting.

- *Tripleurospermum maritimum* subsp. *inodo-rum* 'Bridal Robe' is an ornamental annual related to German chamomile with large, double, white blossoms.

Taylor's Tips

HAPPY COMPANIONS

In addition to its beneficial proper-ties for humans, herbalists believe that chamomile makes a good companion for other plants, often improving their flavor or their yield. Among the plants that chamomile may benefit are mints, onions, cabbages, and cucumbers.

BREWING CHAMOMILE TEA

To brew chamomile tea, steep 1 teaspoon fresh or 2 tea-spoons dried blossoms in a cup of boiling water for at least ½ hour. Strain and enjoy the comforting flavor and gentle scent. ∽

LEMON BALM
Melissa officinalis

Zones: 5–9

Type: Perennial

Light: Full sun to part shade

Size: 2 ft. tall, 2 ft. wide

Interest: Loose, upright clump of textured green leaves with strong lemon scent and a hint of mint

Uses: Aromatic, culinary

A member of the square-stemmed mint family, lemon balm forms a spreading clump of loosely branched, crinkled, green foliage. Small white to pale yellow flowers grow clustered in leaf axils. Lemon balm, however, is grown more for its scent than its looks. Little hairs emitting a lemony fragrance when brushed cover its heart-shaped, scalloped leaves. The plant attracts bees galore. In fact, *Melissa* means "honeybee" in Greek.

HOW TO GROW

In rich, moist, well-drained soil, lemon balm will grow and spread with abandon. In less ideal conditions, its habit is more restrained. Cutting back the spent flowers prevents self-seeding and makes the plants bushier and more attractive. Maintain adequate air circulation around lemon balm to avoid powdery mildew.

HOW TO USE

Dry the intensely fragrant leaves of lemon balm in late summer for potpourris and tea. Rub the fresh, oil-rich leaves on wood as a natural, lemon-scented furniture polish. Or add a cup of fresh leaves to your bathwater for an aromatic, soothing experience. The plant is also a natural insect repellent; rub your skin with lemon balm leaves to help keep bugs away.

Traditionally used as a sedative, in Shakespeare's day lemon balm was dried, cut up, and strewn on the floor for a sweet-smelling home. In the kitchen, the minty, lemon flavor of fresh lemon balm complements fruit and green salads, stuffings, seafood, and vegetables, not to mention liqueurs and wines.

Harvest the entire plant at once, just after you notice flower buds. Cut it to within 2 inches of the ground. It will grow back to provide one or two more complete harvests during the season.

Top Choices

- *M.* 'Aurea' is just as useful but more ornamental than the species. It has bright, gold-variegated leaves accented with green veins.

- *M.* 'All Gold' has golden yellow leaves brushed with rich undertones of green.

FREEZING LEMON BALM

Lemon balm retains a fresher flavor when frozen than when dried, although frozen herbs lose their firm texture when thawed. To freeze:

❶ Wash the leaves and stems, then pat dry.

❷ Arrange the leaves on a baking sheet and place in the freezer section of the refrigerator.

❸ After the leaves have completely frozen, remove them from the freezer and place in plastic freezer bags. Seal, label, and return to the freezer.

❹ Use as needed for teas and other applications.

KEEPING BEES AT HOME

Lemon balm is often used by beekeepers to keep adventurous bees near the hives. The use of the plant for this purpose dates back to the ancient Greeks, who believed that if lemon balm was planted near a beehive, the bees would never leave home. Commenting on this attraction, Pliny wrote, "When bees have stayed away they do find their way back home by it."

PENNYROYAL
Mentha pulegium

Zones: 6–9

Type: Perennial

Light: Full sun to part shade

Size: 6–12 in. tall, with an indefinite spread

Interest: Dense, aromatic ground cover of dark green leaves and small lilac-colored flowers

Uses: Aromatic, culinary, insect repellent

Pennyroyal makes an excellent, noninvasive ground cover for damp, shady areas. Its thick mat of dark green leaves has a potent citronella scent that repels insects. Because of its low, dense habit, pennyroyal works well in rock gardens or between the stepping-stones of garden paths. It even makes an excellent lawn substitute that supports occasional mowing. Little whorls of lilac flowers appear above the small leaves.

HOW TO GROW
Pennyroyal grows best in rich, moist, well-drained soil amended with generous amounts of organic matter. Plant in full sun or part shade and water regularly. Cut back flower heads to keep pennyroyal flat and green, or allow the plants to blossom and let them self-sow. Propagate from cuttings or by root division.

HOW TO USE

The species name, *pulegium,* comes from *pulex,* the Latin word for "flea," in reference to pennyroyal's flea-repelling properties, but it does more than repel fleas. Placed in muslin bags and hung in the closet, pennyroyal repels moths and mice. When rubbed on the skin, it can deter gnats, ticks, flies, chiggers, and mosquitoes. The dried leaves add a fragrant touch to potpourris. The annual American pennyroyal, *Hedeoma pulegioides,* has similar properties and was used for centuries by Native Americans.

CAUTION: *Unlike most other mints, pennyroyal should not be taken internally.*

More Mints

- Hardy and vigorous, M. x *piperita,* peppermint, is the best of all mints for drying and thus most appropriate for use in teas. Its powerfully fragrant leaves also make excellent mint jelly and garnishes. It bears a purple flower spike at the stem tip in late summer to early fall. 'Robert Mitchum' has deep green, nearly black, very ornamental leaves.

- M. *spicata,* spearmint, has wrinkled, deep green leaves with a refreshing, cool flavor. 'Kentucky Colonel' is very aromatic and makes excellent iced tea and mint juleps.

- M. *suaveolens* 'Variegata', pineapple mint, is a handsome plant with green leaves irregularly edged in white. It grows about 3 feet tall, spreads quickly, and has a fruity scent.

CREATE A LAWN OF PENNYROYAL

You will love pennyroyal as a lawn substitute; the mowing requirement is minimal. To create a lawn of pennyroyal:

1 Place divisions or new plants 8 to 10 inches apart in prepared soil in spring or early fall.

2 Keep the transplants watered until well established.

3 Mow on a high setting to enhance pennyroyal's flat, matlike appearance.

PENNYROYAL POTPOURRI

To protect your clothes from hungry moths, try using pennyroyal potpourri. Mix ½ cup cedar shavings; ¼ cup each dried pennyroyal, dried lavender, and chipped orris root; ⅛ cup each whole cloves and lemon peel; and 6 drops cedar oil. Place potpourri in a small bag made from a scrap of fabric and close by tying with a ribbon. Store with your clothing. If you are serious about warding off moths, be very generous with the amount of potpourri you put in the bag. (This recipe makes enough for three 3-inch by 6-inch bags.)

BEE BALM
Monarda didyma

Zones: 4–9

Type: Perennial

Light: Full sun to part shade

Size: 2–4 ft. tall, 3–5 ft. wide

Interest: Moplike whorls of scarlet flowers that attract hummingbirds, bees, and butterflies

Uses: Aromatic, culinary, decorative, medicinal

Bee balm, with its bright red whorls of tubular summer flowers, is a magnet to the eye as well as visiting hummingbirds, bees, and butterflies. Also called Oswego tea, the plant has colorful blossoms held above pointed oval leaves that have a spicy citrus fragrance. Bee balm adds as much interest to the table as it does to the garden. Add the flowers and leaves to salads and hors d'oeuvres, or use it in a vase alone or with other cut flowers.

How to Grow

Native to damp, rich sites of North America, bee balm thrives in moist, fertile soil in full sun or light shade. Clumps of this naturally vigorous plant spread quickly, often doubling in size in a season. To control its spread, plant bee balm in a container sunk into the ground.

As the flowers fade, cut plants back to within a few inches of the ground to control self-seeding and powdery mildew. Divide every few years in spring to rejuvenate clumps.

Bee balm produces plentiful amounts of seeds, but growing it from gathered seeds is a bit of a gamble. Since bees frequently cross-pollinate one type with another, the seeds often produce plants with pale flowers and less aromatic foliage than the parents. Grown from seeds, bee balm will usually flower two years after planting.

HOW TO USE

Bee balm adds a summertime look to fresh bouquets. Use the delicately flavored flowers fresh in salads and as edible garnishes, or dry them for potpourris. Leaves add a pleasing flavor to fruit salads, jellies, and cold drinks. They make a soothing yet invigorating tea that aids digestion.

Top Choices

- *M.* 'Gardenview Scarlet' produces 3-inch flowers of intense scarlet and is also mildew-resistant.

- *M.* 'Marshall's Delight' was developed in Canada, bears abundant, deep pink flowers all summer long, and resists powdery mildew.

- *M.* 'Snow Queen' has large numbers of clean white flowers in summer.

- *M. fistulosa,* wild bergamot, is a North American native with pale lavender flowers. It is less showy, but more drought-tolerant, than *M. didyma,* and is often used for drier sites and wildflower or prairie gardens.

Taylor's Tips

A PLEASANT CUP OF TEA

True bergamot oil, which flavors Earl Grey tea, derives from bergamot oranges, *Citrus aurantium* subsp. *bergamia.* Bee balm, however, is a nice substitute. Put a few fresh bee balm leaves in a cup of hot water along with a tea bag of black tea. Strain and enjoy.

BEE BALM AMERICAN STYLE

Bee balm acquired its other common name, Oswego tea, in colonial times. The Oswego Indians were fond of making a tea from the leaves of bee balm that they gathered in fields and open spaces. They shared their tea with the colonists, who in turn used it as a substitute for the often scarce imported tea.

SWEET CICELY
Myrrhis odorata

Zones: 4–8

Type: Perennial

Light: Part shade

Size: 3 ft. tall, 2 ft. wide

Interest: Fragrant, dark green, ferny summer foliage that turns gold in fall

Uses: Aromatic, culinary, decorative, medicinal

Sweet cicely stands out among shade-loving plants for its abundant, finely divided leaves and flat clusters of white springtime blossoms. After flowering, shiny, 1-inch-long, ribbed, brownish black pods develop. This ornamental fruit adds interest to the garden from summer to fall. Sweet cicely has soft, downy leaves that grow up to 1 foot long and taste like sweet licorice. The entire plant is fragrant—thus the species name, *odorata*. Sweet cicely makes an excellent, tall ground cover for shady sites or woodland edges.

HOW TO GROW

Sweet cicely likes moist, humus-rich soil in part shade in northern areas and deeper shade in southern regions. The plant is long-lived and easy to care for if you remember to water it regularly during hot weather. In ideal conditions, sweet cicely may self-sow abundantly. To propagate, gather the seed heads as the pods begin to dry in late summer and shake them in a paper bag to free the seeds. Collect the best seeds from the bottom of the bag and sow directly in the garden. The seeds must be chilled throughout winter to germinate well, a process called stratification. Even then the seeds may sprout erratically. If you are using starter plants, be sure to transplant them when small. Sweet cicely has a long taproot and does not transplant well once this root reaches the bottom of the pot.

HOW TO USE

All parts of sweet cicely are edible. The green seeds have the most intense flavor and should be used fresh. Eat them like candy or use them in salads or as a sugar substitute in light desserts. Add them to soups, omelettes, and scrambled eggs for an invigorating, fresh flavor. For a tasty change of pace, substitute the seeds for anise or caraway seeds in favorite recipes.

Harvest leaves anytime during the growing season. The foliage makes an attractive garnish and can be added to soups, stews and salads for a light, sweet accent. Dig the roots in fall to use fresh in salads, or boil them to serve as a vegetable. They can also be sliced and steamed. Infuse the crushed green seeds or bruised leaves in boiling water for a sweet, anise-flavored tea that helps digestion.

Taylor's Tips

SWEET CICELY FOR THE BORDER

Large plants such as sweet cicely are sometimes just too big for some herb gardens. Remedy by planting this attractive herb in the back of a shady perennial border. The tall stems and plentiful, ferny leaves make it an excellent background plant for shady places.

COLD STRATIFICATION

Sweet cicely seeds lie dormant until conditions for growth are favorable. Stratification is a process developed to overcome dormancy and allow the seeds to germinate more quickly with a greater chance of survival.

Start by soaking the seeds in water for as long as 24 hours. Next, drop the seeds in a perforated can that also contains moist sand. Bury the can at a depth of 2 feet and leave buried over winter.

As the soil starts to warm in spring, dig up the can and sow the germinated seeds immediately. 🐛

CATNIP
Nepeta cataria

Zones: 3–8

Type: Perennial

Light: Full sun to part shade

Size: 2–4 ft. tall, 3 ft. wide

Interest: Bushy, spreading habit with aromatic leaves and spikes of white flowers

Uses: Aromatic, medicinal

Catnip forms a large, relaxed clump of coarse, gray-green, triangular foliage. Its pungent, minty aroma is nearly irresistible to cats. The leaves and stems are covered with a thin layer of white down. In summer, small spikes of pale white flowers appear atop the stems. Catnip belongs to the mint family and, like other mints, has square stems. The vigorous plants spread by rhizomatous roots and by self-sowing. Catnip can become invasive, if your cats don't eat it all first.

HOW TO GROW
Catnip grows well in average soil in full sun to part shade. This easy-to-grow herb is drought-tolerant, pest- and disease-free, and requires little care. Plants grown in rich, fertile soil can be floppy. All plants, regardless of where they are grown, look tired at the end of the grow-

ing season. Control catnip's spread by pulling out or digging up unwanted plants. To prevent self-sowing, deadhead after flowering. Propagate from seeds in spring, by division, or by transplanting self-sown seedlings.

HOW TO USE

Catnip leaves can be gathered anytime but are most potent when the plant begins to flower. The dried leaves are a wonderful filler for cat toys. Catnip tea has a calming, sedative effect and may alleviate cold symptoms.

CAUTION: *Catnip is not recommended for use during pregnancy.*

Top Choices

- *N. cataria* 'Citriodora' has leaves that emit a sweet, lemony aroma.

- *N.* x *faassenii*, catmint, is the best-behaved species because it is sterile and does not set seeds like its more invasive relatives. Catmint has small gray-green leaves and handsome blue, purple, or white double-lipped flowers held on 5-inch spikes. It blooms in July and, if cut back, will repeat in late August or September. Known as "poor man's lavender," it grows 18 to 20 inches tall and looks terrific along the edge of a path or flower border. It has no medicinal use and is less appealing to cats than *N. cataria*.

Taylor's Tips

CATNIP CONTROL

Catnip is most attractive when kept neatly pruned. To encourage bushiness and more attractive foliage, cut back flower spikes before they bloom. Pruning also keeps catnip from self-sowing.

CATNIP AND REALLY BIG CATS

House cats aren't the only felines that think catnip is something special. Years ago catnip oil was used by trappers to attract mountain lions. Experiments with tigers, lions, and leopards have shown that these large cats also love the herb as much as most house cats do.

SWEET BASIL
Ocimum basilicum

Zones: All

Type: Annual

Light: Full sun

Size: 2–3 ft. tall, 1–2 ft. wide

Interest: Intensely fragrant and delicious dark green foliage

Uses: Aromatic, culinary, medicinal

Fragrance, flavor, and healing properties make sweet basil a favorite plant for herb gardens. Basil has an erect, bushy habit with branching stems of richly aromatic, dark green leaves and small spikes of white or pale purple flowers from summer to fall. In addition to being a mainstay of the herb garden, basil's good looks accent a decorative flower border. It also serves you well in the vegetable garden, where its inclusion can enhance the growth of peppers and tomatoes, while repelling asparagus beetles and other pests.

HOW TO GROW

Basil prefers hot weather, full sun, average to fertile soil, and regular watering. Propagate from seeds sown directly in the garden or started eight weeks before the last frost. Place plants 12 inches apart. Except for Japanese beetles, which can be removed by hand and drowned in soapy water, basil is pest-free. Pinch off growing tips and flower spikes to make the plant bushier and to encourage the production of even more of its tasty leaves.

HOW TO USE

Use just-gathered basil leaves in pestos (see recipe at lower right) and tomato sauces, or snip them into green summer salads for a tasty surprise. Add leaves to hot water to make a tea that relieves nausea, fever, and gas pain. Use dried leaves to add a sweet perfume to potpourri. If you allow basil to set flowers, you can use the spikes for interest and aroma in fresh herbal bouquets.

Top Choices

- O. 'Cinnamon', as the name implies, smells and tastes like cinnamon.

- O. 'Citriodorum', lemon basil, has a clean, lemony smell and tastes great with fish, in vinegars, and in herbal teas.

- O. 'Genovese' is large-leaved and one of the best cultivars for making pesto.

- O. 'Mammoth' has leaves large enough to wrap around food before grilling or baking. It also dries well.

- O. 'Piccolo Verde Fino' has small, fragrant leaves, grows only 8 to 10 inches tall, and looks great in a container or when used as an edging.

- O. 'Purple Ruffles' is a large-leaved, bushy cultivar with lavender flowers and shiny, crinkled, dark purple leaves.

ENJOYING BASIL ALL YEAR LONG

Freeze basil to preserve its pungent taste for later use.

1 To freeze it in water, place 2 cups of basil leaves, tightly packed, into a blender with 1 cup of water. Blend until the mixture is thoroughly chopped.

2 Pour the contents into an ice cube tray and place in the freezer.

3 When frozen, pop the cubes out of the tray and into a labeled plastic freezer bag. Add cubes to casseroles, soups, and sauces as desired.

MAKING PESTO

In a food processor, blend 2 cups fresh basil leaves with 4 tablespoons pine nuts, ½ cup olive oil, and 3 cloves garlic until the mixture is a pasty consistency. Add ½ cup grated Parmesan cheese and blend to the desired consistency. Serve on fettuccine or cooked zucchini, or as a companion to steak.

SWEET MARJORAM
Origanum majorana

Zones: 9–10

Type: Perennial grown as an annual

Light: Full sun

Size: 1–2 ft. tall, 1–2 ft. wide

Interest: Fragrant, gray-green, oval leaves on mounded stems tipped with knots of gray bracts

Uses: Aromatic, culinary, medicinal

Of the three popular marjorams—sweet marjoram, pot marjoram, and wild marjoram—sweet marjoram is the most fragrant and delicious. It forms a low, bushy mound of ¼- to 1-inch-long, gray-green, oval leaves. The small white flowers appear at the stem tips from summer to fall. Knotlike bunches of gray bracts surround the blossoms, the inspiration for its other common name, knotted marjoram. Sweet marjoram, thyme, and basil are often planted together in the garden for their complementary shapes, colors, and fragrances. They are often used together in cooking.

HOW TO GROW
Sweet marjoram likes well-drained soil in full sun. It is not drought-tolerant, however, so amend the soil with plenty of compost before planting and water when

needed. Buy starter plants or sow seeds indoors early in spring. Plant outdoors 8 inches apart after the last frost. For more compact plants and more leaves, pinch the growing tips.

HOW TO USE

A well-known ingredient in Greek, German, and Italian cuisines, marjoram's flowers, leaves, stems, and seeds are all edible. They are prized for the delicate spiciness they add to meats, soups, stews, pasta, and sauces. This herb has also been used for its sedative and antiseptic properties, as well as for an aid to digestion and menstrual irregularity. Try a mellow nightcap of 2 teaspoons of fresh leaves steeped in a cup of boiling water. Sweet marjoram has also been used in perfumes, herbal baths, and sachets.

Top Choices

- *O.* x *majoricum*, hardy sweet marjoram (Italian oregano), forms an 18-inch mound of sharply aromatic, gray-green leaves; it is not as sweet as but is hardier than sweet marjoram. Zones 7 to 10.

- *O. vulgare* subsp. *hirtum* (also classified as *O. heracleoticum*), Greek oregano, is more potent and spicy than sweet marjoram and is the best oregano to use in Italian cooking. It is smaller and less vigorous than wild marjoram. Zones 5 to 10.

- *O. vulgare* subsp. *vulgare*, wild marjoram, commonly sold as oregano, has erect stems and pretty, rosy flowers in late summer. Avoid it for culinary uses, because it has little flavor. Zones 5 to 10.

SWEET MARJORAM AND BUG BITES

Since medieval times, sweet marjoram has been used to relieve the discomfort caused by mosquito and other bug bites.

❶ Gather a handful of sweet marjoram leaves and bruise them with a rolling pin to release the essential oil.

❷ Roll the leaves into a ball and hold the leaves against the bite for 5 to 10 minutes.

BUY IT RIGHT

Plants grown from seeds can be quite variable. To be sure you get the plants you want, buy starter plants in spring from a garden center or order them from a mail-order catalog. To be sure you are getting a fragrant plant, sniff the plant at the garden center before purchasing.

AMERICAN GINSENG
Panax quinquefolius

Zones: 3–8

Type: Perennial

Light: Full shade

Size: 1–2 ft.tall,
1–2 ft. wide

Interest: Dark green
leaves; shiny red
berries following
greenish white flowers

Uses: Decorative,
medicinal

American ginseng is an herb of shady, wooded places. It is a lovely addition to the woodland garden. In spring, a central umbel of greenish white flowers is held above fans of compound, dark green leaves. In summer, a tight cluster of glossy red berries adds a touch of scarlet to the landscape. For over two thousand years, ginseng's man-shaped root has had a magical reputation among herbalists. It has been regarded as one of nature's most powerful herbs, with the ability to confer wisdom and restore youthful vigor to aging bodies.

HOW TO GROW
American ginseng is native to cool, moist, hardwood forests and wooded, north-facing slopes throughout the central and southeastern United States. It is difficult to cultivate but grows best in conditions that mimic its

native habitat: deep deciduous shade and cool, moist soil rich in organic matter. To create these preferred conditions, add a little bonemeal to rich forest soil and mulch with leaf mold. Good drainage is essential to avoid root rot.

In the wild, ginseng seeds take eighteen to twenty-four months to germinate and another five to seven years to mature. If you buy starter plants, it still takes four to six years for a crop. To propagate, sow seeds in the spring, covering them with 1 inch of soil.

HOW TO USE

To harvest, dig up roots of mature plants in fall to use fresh or to dry. Herbalists believe that *P. quinquefolius* helps everything from stress and fatigue to concentration and convalescence. Steep the roots in boiling water to make a relaxing, sweet, and earthy tea.

Top Choices

- Practitioners of traditional Chinese medicine prize *P. quinquefolius,* American ginseng, as a cure-all, tonic, and aphrodisiac as well as for its beneficial effects on children and adults under forty years old.

- *P. ginseng,* ginseng, has properties similar to American ginseng. It is traditionally taken for old-age complaints and to increase vitality, but is not recommended for children.

GINSENG IMITATORS

The umbrella-like canopy of ginseng's foliage adds a note of distinctive beauty to open forest landscapes. It is, however, not the easiest plant to grow if an airy ground cover is what you need. Wild sarsaparilla, *Aralia nudicaulis,* is an alternative to ginseng.

Native to open hardwood and mixed conifer-hardwood forests of the northeastern United States, wild sarsaparilla plants often form umbrella-shaped leaf canopies similar to ginseng. However, they are much more vigorous and also more forgiving of the occasional misstep.

The plant's knee-high foliage hides a fuzzy white spring flower and dark blue late-summer berries. The aromatic root has the faint odor of sarsaparilla.

Wild sarsaparilla does not have the herbal healing qualities attributed to ginseng, but the dried roots are sometimes used to brew a pleasant tea.

PASSIONFLOWER
Passiflora incarnata

Zones: 6–10

Type: Perennial

Light: Full sun to part shade

Size: Vine 15–30 ft. tall

Interest: Fragrant, showy lavender flowers followed by edible, egg-sized yellow fruit

Uses: Decorative, medicinal

Passionflower is as useful as its flowers are spectacular. Native to southern North America, passionflower bears scented, 2- to 3-inch-wide, light purple to white summer blooms. The vigorous vines climb by means of curly tendrils and quickly cover fences and other supports. The medium green, deeply lobed leaves make a bitter-tasting tea that calms the nerves and relieves anxiety. When fully ripe, the fruit is sweetly aromatic and is delightful when used fresh in fruit salads.

HOW TO GROW
Passionflower likes a warm, sunny location in well-drained, sandy soil. Extra water and a little shade help it grow its best in very warm regions. In northern areas, it makes an excellent container plant that is easily over-

wintered indoors. Propagate from seeds in spring or cuttings in summer.

The passionflower vine climbs by wrapping tendrils around supports such as shrubs, trellises, chicken wire, and lazy gardeners. Cut it back in late winter or early spring before new growth appears. Planted in the ground, passionflower produces many suckers that should be thinned in late fall or winter. Mulch for winter protection.

Passionflower is sometimes troubled by thrips and mealybugs, as well as by cucumber mosaic virus, which mottles the foliage and stunts growth. Remove diseased plants immediately and keep the area around the plant weed-free, because some weeds serve as hosts for the virus. Spray insecticidal soap on infested plants to control insects.

HOW TO USE

The fruit of passionflower has many seeds embedded in its sweet, succulent pulp, which is delicious when used fresh in desserts or jams. Unfortunately, only gardeners in warm climates can enjoy the fruit, because it ripens in fall and cannot fully mature before being killed by frost in cold-climate gardens. The stems and leaves contain sedating, nonaddictive properties, so they are often brewed into a calming tea.

Top Choices

- *P. caerulea*, blue passionflower, bears striking purple and white flowers, followed by orange fruit. Zones 8 to 10.

- *P.* x *alatocaerulea*, passionvine, grows quickly to 20 feet tall with large, fragrant flowers all summer. Zones 7 to 10.

MYTHS OF THE PASSIONFLOWER

Spanish missionaries considered passionflower a good omen because the structure of its 2- to 3-inch, fragrant, lavender flowers recalled to them Christ's Passion.

The ten faithful apostles (Judas and Peter are excluded), the whip, the spear, the nails and hammer, Christ's five wounds, and the crown of thorns are symbolically represented in the petals, sepals, tendrils, leaves and pistil, stamens, and corolla, respectively. Thus, the name *Passiflora* means "the flower of the Passion," and the common name has a similar meaning.

Whatever one's beliefs, however, passionflower makes a stunning addition to gardens in warm-weather zones and a beautiful indoor vine everywhere.

SCENTED GERANIUM
Pelargonium

Zones: All

Type: Tender perennial grown as an annual

Light: Full sun

Size: Variable height and width

Interest: Strongly scented leaves and delicate white, pink, or lavender flowers

Uses: Aromatic, culinary

Gardeners marvel at the intense and varied fragrances of scented geraniums. Some of them—for example, lemon-scented *Pelargonium crispum*—need only a touch to release their aroma. The rich fragrance of others, such as rose-scented *P. graveolens*, is readily apparent. Nutmeg geranium has trailing stems suitable for hanging baskets; peppermint geranium, *P. tomentosum*, boasts fuzzy silver leaves on stems up to 4 feet tall. The variety 'Chocolate Mint' has gray-green leaves accented with brown, and it has a sweet, minty fragrance. Both of these look lovely in a pot or spilling over a retaining wall.

HOW TO GROW
Scented geraniums require well-drained, evenly moist soil in full sun for maximum fragrance. If grown in small

containers, water when the top of the soil is dry. If the pot is large, stick your finger at least an inch into the soil to check for dryness. Too much watering leads to soilborne diseases and root rot, while too little turns the leaves yellow.

Fertilize with a water-soluble fertilizer at half strength every other watering during the growing season. Every fourth time you fertilize, add a teaspoon of Epsom salts to a gallon of the fertilizer solution to supply the magnesium needed by scented geraniums.

HOW TO USE

Although the flowers are short-lived, the foliage of this herb lives for weeks, retaining a handsome appearance and fragrance. Rose, lemon, and mint varieties add flavor to many recipes. Candy the leaves with egg white and extra-fine sugar (see page 23). Rose geraniums add flavor to sugar, jelly, cake, icing, sorbet, and herbal tea and vinegar. Dry the leaves for potpourri.

Top Choices

- *P. capitatum* 'Attar of Roses' is excellent for sachets and potpourris.

- *P. citronellum* (formerly 'Mabel Grey') has two-toned pink flowers, coarse leaves, and a powerful lemon fragrance.

- *P. odoratissimum* smells like sweet apple cider and has soft, long, trailing stems that look handsome spilling over the edges of pots or hanging baskets.

PROPAGATION FROM CUTTINGS

Many herbs, from mint to scented geraniums (pictured above), can be easily propagated from transplanted stem cuttings.

1 Pinch a 4-inch-long stem just beneath a set of leaves. Cut the end with a sharp knife and remove the lowest set of leaves from the stem.

2 Fill a clean pot with moist potting mix and poke a 2-inch-deep hole in the soil.

3 Insert the cutting in the hole and gently firm the soil around the stem.

4 Keep in a warm spot in filtered light and mist daily. Cuttings of most herbs will root in a month or two. Rooted cuttings can be overwintered as houseplants.

CURLED PARSLEY
Petroselinum crispum

Zones: All

Type: Biennial grown as an annual

Light: Full sun to part shade

Size: 1 ft. tall, 1 ft. wide

Interest: Rosettes of curly, dark green leaves with flat umbels of yellowish green flowers in the second year

Uses: Culinary

Curled parsley's crisp foliage garnishes everything from a platter of deviled eggs at a casual backyard barbecue to a slab of grilled salmon at a fancy restaurant. Parsley is a nutritious food, high in iron and vitamins A, C, and E. It's also quite tasty, adding a mild but distinctive flavor to many foods. With its divided, curly leaves crimped at the margins, this herb looks as charming edging a flower bed as it does garnishing a tray of hors d'oeuvres. The tidy plant bears flat clusters of greenish yellow flowers in its second summer, followed by small, ribbed, oval seeds.

HOW TO GROW
Parsley is easy to grow but the seeds are slow to germinate; if you'd rather not wait, buy small starter plants for your garden at a nursery instead. This herb prefers moist,

well-drained soil with plenty of organic matter and a location with part shade to full sun. To boost germination, soak seeds overnight in warm water. Sow indoors eight weeks before the last frost. Plant seedlings 8 inches apart. Start harvesting when plants are 6 or 7 inches tall, taking the older outer leaves to allow for new leaf growth in the center. A somewhat less reliable method of propagation is to let a plant go to seed in your garden and hope it will self-sow, rewarding you the following spring with numerous seedlings.

HOW TO USE

Parsley can be eaten fresh, dried, or frozen. Use it as a garnish or chop it and mix it with food just before serving. As a biennial, parsley flowers the second year on 3-foot stems. Its foliage tastes bitter the second year, so grow new plants each spring for a steady supply of fresh, young, leaves. Flat-leaved parsley has a stronger flavor and is better for cooking than the curly-leaved varieties.

Top Choices

- *P.* 'Catalogno' and 'Italian', like other flat-leaved parsleys, have a much stronger flavor than curly-leaved varieties but are not as decorative.
- *P.* var. *tuberosum,* Hamburg parsley, is grown for its long fleshy root that looks like a parsnip and is eaten as a vegetable. Although its foliage is nutritious, it lacks the flavor of curled parsley.

Taylor's Tips

KEEP IT COLD

- For long-lasting freshness and crispness, stand stems of parsley in cold water for several hours.

- Add fresh, chopped, flat-leaved parsley to sauces, salads, and stews shortly before serving.

- To freeze parsley for later use, put the leaves in a food processor and run until finely chopped. Place the parsley bits on a tray in the freezer. When frozen, put the loose, chopped parsley in a plastic container, seal tightly, and store in the freezer until needed.

PLANT EXTRA
PARSLEY

Parsley is one of the most recognizable of the culinary herbs. Unfortunately, it is also irresistible to the parsley worm, a small yellow and green caterpillar with black stripes. It is worth your while to fight the urge to kill this insect, because the ravaging pest will become a beautiful (and endangered) black swallowtail butterfly. Plan ahead for this possibility by planting enough parsley to satisfy you and the caterpillars.

COWSLIP

Primula veris

Zones: 5–8

Type: Perennial

Light: Sun in spring, shade in summer

Size: 6 in. tall, 6 in. wide

Interest: Fragrant yellow flowers and rich green, oblong leaves

Uses: Culinary, decorative, medicinal

Cowslip is an attractive, low-growing, perennial wildflower of England and continental Europe that has become a popular addition to North American gardens. The plant forms a basal rosette of soft, crinkled, ovate, gray-green leaves. In early spring, downy, 6-inch stems rise from the center, topped by umbels of deep yellow, slightly nodding flowers. The fragrant blooms have orange-spotted throats surrounded by five petals. Cowslip is charming at the edge of a shady path or border, or in masses in woodland gardens or rockeries.

HOW TO GROW

Cowslip prefers full sun to part shade in spring and full shade in summer. Plant in spring in well-drained soil generously amended with organic matter, topped with mulch. Propagate cowslip by division after flowers have faded in late spring to early summer. You can also collect the ripe seeds, sowing them immediately after gathering, or let the plants self-sow. Cowslip grows particularly well in the Pacific Northwest, where the cool summers and mild winters are similar to those of England.

Remove slugs and snails by hand, and aphids and spider mites by spraying with water or insecticidal soap.

HOW TO USE

Cowslip flowers are rich in sweet nectar—a treat to people, butterflies, and humming-birds alike. Sprinkle fresh blossoms in salads for a colorful touch, or brew the fresh or dried flowers into a calming tea to soothe headaches and calm nerves. Cowslip is a traditional ingredient in syrups, vinegars, and country wines.

Ornamental Primrose

- *P. veris* is a parent of *P.* x *polyantha*, polyanthus primrose, which is one of the most popular and easy to grow of the garden primroses. Hardy to Zone 3, it stands 8 to 12 inches tall and grows equally wide. The rose-scented flowers come in a wide range of colors and combinations, including solids and two-tones with yellow eyes. In warm climates, they can be used as winter-flowering annuals.

FAIRY CAPS AND COWSLIPS

Cowslip is as English as are kings and queens. Of cowslip's many common names, a number stem from English fables and traditions about the plant. For example, the name *fairy cap* derives from the belief that cowslip was a favorite flower of fairies, the diminutive folk thought to inhabit glens and thickets throughout the wild English countryside.

Other names such as keyflower and key of heaven come from the resemblance of cowslip's flower bud clusters to a key ring crowded with keys, one of the symbols of Saint Peter.

Polyanthus primroses are easy-to-grow, tidy plants with a sweet fragrance that is the essence of spring.

LUNGWORT
Pulmonaria officinalis

Zones: 3–9

Type: Perennial

Light: Light to full shade

Size: 1½ ft. tall, 1½ ft. wide

Interest: Pink and blue flowers followed by large, light green leaves splashed with white

Uses: Culinary, decorative

This attractive, noninvasive ground cover brightens shady spots with colorful, pastel pink and blue flowers and dramatic, white-splashed leaves. Lungwort also makes a pretty edging for a shaded path and can perk up a dark corner of the garden. The flowers are deep pink as they open and fade to blue before they drop. Not all leaves of lungwort bear the typical white splotches.

How to Grow

Lungwort thrives in moist, peaty soil in light to full shade and tolerates heavy clay soil. It is a clump-forming perennial that spreads slowly by rhizomes. Propagate lungwort by division in fall. It also self-sows when grown in favorable conditions. Pick off sawfly larvae if they attack the leaves, or spray affected plants with neem oil, a tree-derived insecticide. Slugs, which can also be a problem, are fond of beer. Pour some in a shallow container and set it in the ground near your plant. The slugs fall in and drown when they stop by for a drink. If the foliage becomes damaged, cut the plant back, and it will grow new leaves.

HOW TO USE

Cut lungwort flowers for spring bouquets, or flavor a salad with the fresh new leaves. In years past, herbalists claimed the herb had expectorant properties, and it was taken internally for coughs, bronchitis, and other conditions affecting the lungs. Vermouth often contains a lungwort extract. The best leaves for herbal purposes are young and fresh, so pick them early in the season to dry for later use.

Top Choices

- *P.* 'Sissinghurst White' is a cultivar with white flowers and light green, spotted leaves.

- *P. longifolia* 'Bertram Anderson' is distinguished by its violet-blue flowers and its long, narrow, green leaves spotted with silver. Zones 5 to 8.

- *P. saccharata* 'Mrs. Moon' is one of the prettiest and most popular lungworts. Its dark green leaves have irregular white splotches. The long-lasting flowers open pink and turn sky blue in spring. Zones 3 to 8.

THE DOCTRINE OF SIGNATURES

Lungwort's common and botanical names refer to its traditional reputation as a cure for lung diseases, a treatment now considered of questionable benefit.

Lungwort's former status as a pulmonary cure resulted from the likeness of its randomly splotched leaves to diseased lung tissue, a connection that followed the Doctrine of Signatures. The doctrine, advocated by Paracelsus (d. 1541), said that the way a plant looked determined which parts of the body it could heal.

With its white flowers and decorative leaves, P. 'Sissinghurst White' is a favorite choice to brighten dull, shady spots in the herb garden.

APOTHECARY'S ROSE
Rosa gallica 'Officinalis'

Zones: 3–8

Type: Perennial shrub

Light: Full sun

Size: 3 ft. tall, 3 ft. wide

Interest: Fragrant, semi-double, deep pink flowers with gold stamens; crinkled, medium green leaves

Uses: Aromatic, culinary, decorative, medicinal

Apothecary's rose combines beauty and delicious scent with winter hardiness and disease resistance to make it a must-grow plant in the flower border or herb garden. It flowers heavily for four to five weeks in summer, producing deep pink, semidouble, fragrant blooms with gold stamens, followed by round red fruit (hips) in fall. It freely suckers when grown on its own roots, making it suitable for planting on banks as a ground cover. You can purchase grafted plants that do not produce suckers. These plants mature into attractive, 3- to 4-foot, compact shrubs.

HOW TO GROW

Apothecary's rose needs full sun to ensure maximum bloom. Plant in early spring or fall in a sheltered location with plenty of morning sun to dry the dew from the leaves. In southern areas, some light afternoon shade protects the plants from extreme heat. Soil should be slightly acidic, very well drained, and should contain plenty of organic matter.

For grafted plants, set the bud union 2 inches below the soil surface in cold climates and at ground level in warm areas. Fertilize apothecary's rose once in early spring with dehydrated cow manure and bonemeal, or use a commercial fertilizer for roses. Regular, generous watering early in the day and good air circulation help prevent powdery mildew and black spot on the leaves. If aphids appear, spray with insecticidal soap.

HOW TO USE

Apothecary's rose was used to treat everything from colds and infections to skin problems and depression. Herbalists claim rose water or rose oil (attar of roses) in skin-care products soothes the skin; aromatherapists believe that the fragrance relieves anxiety. It's also a beautiful cut flower, with a lovely floral fragrance that quickly fills a room. When dried, the petals are an excellent choice for conserves and potpourris. Add fresh petals to salads, candy them (see page 23), or use in syrups and jellies.

Top Choices

- *R.* 'Rosa Mundi' bears stunning semi-double flowers striped with bands of scarlet and white. The flowers are wonderfully fragrant and can be used just like apothecary's rose.

A ROSY CONCOCTION

Rose petal honey has long been used to soothe scratchy throats irritated by coughs. This delicately flavored concoction is not just for the sickroom, however; it adds a warm touch of nostalgia to herbal teas. It is also delightful drizzled over hot waffles or pancakes. To make rose petal honey:

1 Pick about ⅔ ounce of rose petals from flowers that are not yet fully open.

2 Stir the petals into 4 ounces of honey and heat over a low flame until the mixture begins to bubble.

3 Strain the honey and store in the refrigerator in a clean, tightly sealed glass container.

AVOIDING MILDEW

Roses are particularly susceptible to powdery mildew. To keep this fungus at bay, do not plant apothecary's rose in a dry site. Water and mulch regularly. If you discover a little telltale white powder on the leaves, do not panic. Remove the infected leaves and discard.

ROSEMARY
Rosmarinus officinalis

Zones: 8–10

Type: Perennial some-times grown as an annual

Light: Full sun

Size: 1–4 ft. tall, 1–4 ft. wide

Interest: Fragrant, evergreen foliage and blue to white flowers that attract bees

Uses: Aromatic, culinary, decorative, medicinal

Rosemary, with its needlelike leaves and potent fragrance, is one of the most useful and versatile herbs. As a kitchen seasoning, the leaves are used for flavoring many recipes. In mild climates, it can grow to 4 feet tall; in cooler climates, where it is treated as an annual or wintered indoors, it tends to be smaller. Its thick foliage can be shaped into a formal hedge or a standard, a slender trunk topped with a sphere of evergreen foliage. Rosemary begins blooming in late winter on old wood and continues into spring with two-lipped flowers in shades of pale blue, lilac, or white.

HOW TO GROW
Rosemary grows best in well-drained, slightly moist soil. Set plants about 2 feet apart for an upright hedge, or use the prostrate form, also spaced 2 feet apart, to create

a fragrant ground cover. To keep plants compact, cut back after blooming. You can also pinch the growing tips to promote bushiness.

Grow rosemary from seeds or take stem cuttings from new wood in spring and remove the bottom leaves. Place the cuttings in damp sand or water until roots appear. When planted outdoors, rosemary is pest-free. Indoors, it is susceptible to houseplant pests such as aphids, mealybugs, and spider mites. To combat these, spray the plants regularly with a weak solution of Murphy's Oil™ Soap and water.

HOW TO USE

The intense, resinous flavor of rosemary tastes delicious with meat, chicken, seafood, vegetables, soups, breads, and sauces. Use whole sprigs (remove before serving) as a light accent to recipes, or try minced fresh leaves for a more robust flavor. Rosemary tea may make you sleepy. To brew it, steep 1 teaspoon of dried rosemary or 3 teaspoons of fresh flowers and leaves per cup of boiling water. Herbalists say that rosemary eases gas pains and headaches, aids eyesight and memory, and helps keep hair and complexion healthy.

Top Choices

- *R.* 'Arp', the hardiest rosemary cultivar, is hardy to Zone 7 or, in a protected location, to Zone 6.

- *R.* 'Prostratus' is a low-growing, creeping rosemary good for edging a rock garden or as ground cover. It's also nice in a hanging basket.

OVERWINTERING ROSEMARY

In cold climates, rosemary can be overwintered indoors in a cool, sunny spot. To encourage blooms indoors, keep the plant very cool.

1 Dig up the plant in early fall before the first frost. Knock excess dirt from the rootball.

2 Repot in pasteurized potting soil, making sure the plant has excellent drainage. Prune out any damaged branches.

3 Water regularly but do not overwater during the winter. Stick your finger into the soil 1 inch deep and test for dryness. In warm rooms with low humidity, spritz with water daily to keep the leaves from drying out.

4 Snip stems as needed for use in cooking.

SAGE
Salvia officinalis

Zones: 5–8

Type: Perennial

Light: Full sun

Size: 2 ft. tall,
2 ft. wide

Interest: Soft, fragrant,
gray-green leaves and
blue-purple flowers

Uses: Aromatic, culinary, decorative,
medicinal

Sage, a member of the mint family, is a beautiful plant with downy, wrinkled, gray-green leaves. It is graced with blue-purple summertime flowers. The blossoms, which attract bees, are two-lipped and grow in four to eight false whorls at axils along the stem tips. The long-stemmed leaves hang gracefully from the stems and have a spicy aroma. Ancient herbalists believed that eating the herb could slow the aging process and sharpen the memory. Sage, which means "wise," has become a symbol of wisdom and immortality.

HOW TO GROW
Native to the Mediterranean and North Africa, sage can tolerate poor soil but needs good drainage to thrive, a trait that makes it excellent for containers and raised beds. It is prone to root rot in wet conditions.

In warm climates, sage is evergreen; in cold areas, the plants die back in winter and need spring pruning for healthy new growth. Divide garden sage every few years, and replace it when the stems grow both hard and woody. Plant rooted cuttings in pots and overwinter indoors on a sunny windowsill.

Tender species, such as pineapple sage, can be propagated the same way, overwintered indoors, and then planted in the garden in spring. Sage can also be propagated by seeds or layering.

HOW TO USE

The appealing, slightly musky taste of sage leaves adds flavorful depth to meat, poultry, fish, soups, and many vegetables. Sage also makes fatty meats more digestible. For the strongest flavor, cook with dried leaves. To prepare sage for use as a seasoning, grind fresh leaves in a food mill or rub dried leaves through a fine screen. The crushed, dried leaves make a refreshing tea.

Top Choices

- *S. elegans*, pineapple sage, has red flowers and a pineapple scent, making it a good choice for such diverse uses as tea, salad, and potpourri. Zones 4 to 10.

- *S. officinalis* 'Tricolor' has variegated, aromatic leaves in shades of white, purple, and green. Zones 7 to 10.

- *S. sclarea* (also called *S. hormonium*), clary sage, is an aromatic biennial used for potpourris and for seasoning food and drink. The flowers are tasty in salads and make a soothing tea. Zones 4 to 10.

MAKING PLANTS BUSHIER

After your plant has reached 6 inches high, pinch back the growing tip at the top of the plant. When new shoots appear along the sides, use your thumb and index finger to pinch out the tips of the new side stems to encourage a more compact, bushier plant.

If you let the plant flower, pinch off dead blooms so the plant puts its energy into making more stems, flowers, and foliage instead of setting seeds.

SUMMER SAVORY
Satureja hortensis

Zones: All

Type: Annual

Light: Full sun

Size: 1–2 ft. tall, 1–2 ft. wide

Interest: Scented, narrow, pointed leaves and two-lipped lilac or white flowers that attract bees

Uses: Culinary

The narrow green leaves of summer savory resemble rosemary but have a tangy flavor all their own. Ancient herbalists attributed increased sex drive to summer savory (and the opposite to winter savory). Today, the reputation of summer savory lies with its peppery taste, which adds delicate spiciness to many meat and vegetable dishes. The plant forms a relaxed mound of slender, hairy, 12- to 18-inch-tall stems covered with narrow gray-green leaves. A member of the mint family, savory bears small groups of white or lilac flowers in the upper leaf axils. The blossoms, leaves, and stems are all aromatic.

The botanical name, *Satureja*, derives from the Greek word for "satyr" and refers to the herb's old-time use as an aphrodisiac.

HOW TO GROW

Sun-loving summer savory needs dry, sandy soil with excellent drainage. You can grow this annual equally well indoors in a container or outdoors in the garden. Propagate from cuttings or seeds. Sow the seeds, which germinate quickly, either indoors in flats four to six weeks before the last frost or directly in the garden where you want the plants to grow. Thin seedlings so they are 6 to 10 inches apart.

HOW TO USE

Summer savory tastes good either fresh or dried, served with beans and vegetables, and in herb butters, vinegars, soups, and teas. It makes a quite pleasant digestive tea, which can also relieve diarrhea. The flavor of summer savory is strongest just before the plant begins to flower, so that is a good time to harvest it.

Winter Savory

- *S. montana,* winter savory, grows in similar conditions to summer savory, but it is perennial to Zone 6. Winter savory's flavor is stronger and more resinous than that of summer savory. Winter savory forms a low, 1-foot-tall and 2-foot-wide mound of shiny evergreen leaves. Abundant whorls of small white, lavender, or pink flowers attract bees in late summer. Zones 6 to 10.

AN AROMATIC GARDEN

One of the challenges facing some homeowners is how to turn a dry, gravelly slope into an attractive part of the yard. You can create a beautiful herb garden and control erosion at the same time.

Some herbs, such as winter savory, lavender, sage, rosemary, and thyme, thrive in sandy soils and prefer to grow on dry hillsides where they are native.

1 Set transplants of these five plants on the dry slope, spacing them 18 inches apart.

2 Plant the herbs and mulch lightly with an inorganic mulch like washed gravel.

3 Water regularly until established. The plants will not only lend beauty to the hillside, but fill the surrounding air with their spicy aromas as well.

MEXICAN MINT MARIGOLD
Tagetes lucida

Zones: 8–10

Type: Perennial grown as an annual

Light: Full sun to part shade

Size: 3 ft. tall, 3 ft. wide

Interest: Bushy clump of aromatic foliage and single, yellow flowers

Uses: Aromatic, culinary

A rich licorice aroma permeates the leaves, stems, and flowers of Mexican mint marigold. The plant has erect stems and narrow, lance-shaped leaves about 3/4 inch long. Mexican mint marigold bears single, deep yellow blooms at the ends of the stems. In colder climates, where it is grown as an annual for its fragrant foliage, it develops few flowers. In hot climates, it is a good substitute for French tarragon.

HOW TO GROW
Mexican mint marigold needs a long, hot growing season and plenty of sun to bloom its best. Pinch the growing tips for a fuller plant. In northern areas, plant seeds 6 weeks before the last frost. From Zone 9 south, sow seeds outdoors anytime. Set plants 1 foot apart. Mexican mint marigold is pest- and disease-free.

HOW TO USE

Mexican mint marigold tea contains vitamin C and phosphorus and is used as a nutritious tonic. Brew it from the petals alone or from whole dried flowers and leaves. Add dried flowers and leaves to potpourris, or use them fresh or dried in cooking as a substitute for French tarragon. Mexican mint marigold may help improve digestion, lower fevers, and relieve anxiety. When burned, the plant's aroma repels insects. Applied to skin, it works as a tick remover.

Top Choices

Use these species and varieties in the same way you would Mexican mint marigold—in teas, fresh salads, and potpourris.

- *T. patula*, French marigold, is an aromatic, compact, bushy annual often used for bedding or edging. It flowers from early summer to frost with single or double flowers ranging in color from red and mahogany to yellow, orange, and bicolors.

- *T. tenuifolia* 'Lemon Gem' has edible leaves and flowers with a lemony scent. The plant bears abundant, single blossoms of clear yellow and makes an excellent edging or container plant. Use flowers in potpourris, or candy them to decorate desserts.

Taylor's Tips

BENEFICIAL PLANTING STRATEGY

Avoid planting French marigolds near beans because the marigolds may stunt their growth. The same marigolds, however, are beneficial allies of many other plants, from lovely roses to tasty tomatoes.

- Marigolds may repel nematodes, Mexican bean beetles, and Colorado potato beetles.

- Planting French marigolds between cabbages helps repel cabbage looper butterflies.

- Underplant tomatoes and roses with French marigolds to keep aphids in check. Marigolds attract hover flies, which in turn eat aphids.

MULCHING MADE EASY

Cut Mexican mint marigold to the ground and cover with mulch after a hard frost. Before mulching, be sure to remove nearby weeds. As winter gives way to spring, remove the mulch to allow the cold to escape. When spring is firmly established, apply a summer mulch to help warm the soil further. ❧

GERMANDER
Teucrium chamaedrys

Zones: 5–9

Type: Perennial

Light: Full sun to part shade

Size: 1 ft. tall, 1 ft. wide

Interest: Small, glossy, aromatic leaves and spikes of pink flowers that attract bees

Uses: Decorative

A member of the mint family, germander has square stems covered with oval green leaves just 1 inch long. Actually, germander is like a miniature version of boxwood, with a low, mounded habit and neat, shiny leaves on woody stems that lend themselves to shearing. During summer, unsheared germander produces stalks of showy, bright purple flowers that attract bees to the garden. Once considered a medicinal herb, germander is now used as an ornamental plant in herb gardens and evergreen shrub borders.

HOW TO GROW
Germander prefers full sun and well-drained, slightly acidic, average soil. Plant in a sheltered location to avoid wind damage to the evergreen foliage. Provide winter protection in the North with mulch or burlap barriers.

Propagate germander from seeds or by layering or division in spring. Be patient—it takes germander seeds about a month to germinate. Alternatively, you can propagate from stem cuttings early in the growing season. When growing the herb outdoors, space plants about 12 inches apart or grow them in containers. Germander is pest-free, and heat- and drought-resistant. Spring is the best time to shear germander hedges and prune older plants to encourage new, vigorous growth.

HOW TO USE

Germander makes a handsome, aromatic edging for modern herbal knot gardens, highlighting their geometric shapes. Applied externally, germander helps heal diseased gums and, in the past, was a treatment for snakebites and skin problems. It is used to flavor vermouths and liqueurs. Germander's attractive foliage and strong stems make it useful for simple topiaries and crafts such as dried or living herbal wreaths.

Top Choices

- *T. marum,* cat thyme, is about 1 foot tall and looks like thyme. The plants have abundant gray-green, very aromatic leaves. The fragrance of the foliage can be overpowering, but cats love it. Zones 8 to 10.

- *T. scorodonia,* wood sage, has leaves with the aroma of hops, for which it can substitute in beer-making. It stands up to 1 foot tall and bears yellow flowers in summer.

MAKING A STANDARD

To make a standard, begin with a small potted transplant.

1 Set a stake in the pot about an inch away from the stem.

2 Tie the strongest stem to the stake and remove all other stems.

3 As the stem grows, remove all side shoots that develop.

4 When the stem reaches the desired height, allow side shoots to develop, pinching them back lightly to encourage branching.

5 Continue pinching until you have created a spherical mound of foliage. Trim as needed to maintain the desired shape.

THYME
Thymus vulgaris

Zones: 4–9

Type: Perennial

Light: Full sun

Size: 12 in. tall,
8 in. wide

Interest: Aromatic
gray-green leaves and
lilac flowers that
attract bees

Uses: Culinary, decorative, medicinal

Highly acclaimed for its strong, pungent taste, garden thyme enhances the flavor of meats, breads, and vegetables. Of all the thymes, this is the most flavorful. It has an upright habit with pink to lilac flowers in the axils of the stem tips. A highly respected member of the mint family, it looks and smells delightful in herbal wreaths. Thyme makes an attractive edging or ground cover in the herb garden. Planted throughout a vegetable garden, it may repel pests such as cabbage worms. Bees make flavorful honey from its summertime flowers.

HOW TO GROW
Thyme grows best in full sun and light, well-drained soil. This pest-free Mediterranean native tolerates heat and drought, but it does poorly in wet soil or shade.

A southern exposure or raised bed provides the most favorable growing conditions. Keep areas around plants weeded, and mulch with a nonabsorbent mulch such as sand or gravel to inhibit disease. Over-winter plants beneath a blanket of pine branches. Cut back in early spring to remove woody stems, and after flowering to stimulate growth and prevent self-seeding. Pinch back stems to encourage a bushier habit. Propagate from seeds or cuttings or by division.

HOW TO USE

Thyme leaves taste stronger dried than fresh. Thyme is a basic component in a *bouquet garni,* along with parsley, sweet bay, rosemary, and other herbs. Use it with meats, fish, eggs, and vegetables and in sauces, stews, soups, gumbos, and breads. Thyme tea may prevent nightmares and soothe headaches and hangovers. Syrup made of thyme and honey is good for sore throats and colds.

Top Choices

- *T.* x *citriodorus* 'Bertram Anderson', a form of lemon thyme, makes a mound of shiny yellow-green leaves with a strong lemon aroma. Zones 5 to 9.

- *T. pseudolanuginosus,* woolly thyme, forms a flat, dense mat of fuzzy silver-gray leaves. Zones 5 to 9.

- *T. serpyllum* 'Mother of Thyme', is a vigorous ground cover with pink to lavender flowers and scented leaves.

PLANTING A STRAWBERRY JAR

❶ Fill the jar with potting soil to the level of the first holes.

❷ Set the transplants so the roots are spread on top of the soil and the stems and leaves poke through the holes.

❸ When all plants are set, fill the jar to the next hole level and repeat steps 1 and 2.

JAZZING UP YOUR JELLY

Add fresh thyme leaves to your favorite jelly recipe for added pungency and flavor. Use ¼ cup thyme to 3 cups grape or apple juice. ❧

NASTURTIUM
Tropaeolum majus

Zones: All

Type: Annual

Light: Full sun to part shade

Size: 1 ft. tall, 2 ft. wide

Interest: Round leaves and cheerful red, orange, yellow, or bi-color flowers

Uses: Culinary, decorative

Nasturtiums taste as good as they look. The showy leaves and colorful flowers have a sharp, peppery flavor similar to watercress. The flat, rounded leaves have an attractive, radiating pattern of light green veins. Nasturtiums grow fast and are easy to propagate and maintain. The seeds are large, making them ideal for children to plant. The cheery plants look wonderful covering a bank, spilling over a stone wall, tied to a trellis, or climbing a garden fence. Wherever you grow nasturtium, you won't be disappointed. It adds a wonderful splash of color and peppery taste to many dishes.

HOW TO GROW

Nasturtium is easy to please and thrives in ordinary soil with regular watering. Do not fertilize—in rich soil you will get more leaves than flowers. Nasturtium tolerates both part shade and full sun. Plant the seeds 6 to 12 inches apart and cover with ½ inch of soil. Nasturtium seeds germinate quickly and the plants spread fast but are not invasive. Although subject to aphids, nasturtium is otherwise pest-free. It may self-sow, but seedlings can be lifted easily and moved to another location.

How to Use

The leaves, flowers, and seeds of nasturtiums are high in vitamin C and useful in cooking and medicine. Flowers, buds, and leaves add spiciness and beauty to salads. As an hors d'oeuvre or luncheon dish, the flowers look and taste delicious stuffed with a blend of cream cheese and minced nasturtium leaves. Leaves also enhance cheese and egg dishes. The unripened seeds can be pickled and used as a substitute for capers.

Top Choices

- *T.* 'Empress of India' is an 8-inch-tall dwarf with a bushy habit and small purplish green leaves. Its bright, fragrant, 2-inch-wide, scarlet flowers look charming spilling over the edge of a patio container.

- *T.* 'Alaska' is another 8-inch dwarf useful for edging or containers. It has green-and-white variegated leaves; the flowers show up in a variety of hot colors.

- *T.* 'Butter Cream' bears creamy yellow, semidouble flowers on mounded plants.

- *T.* 'Creamsicle' has orange flowers marked with swirls of creamy white. This charming variety doesn't taste like a Creamsicle, but it looks just as good.

Nasturtiums in Containers

Nasturtiums make excellent container plants, are easy to grow, and look great for months.

Sow the seeds in a window box or other container in well-drained potting mix. Keep the soil moist, and the plants will do the rest.

Soon you will see colorful, helmet-shaped flowers waving over shield-shaped foliage. (The source of the genus name is *tropaion*, the Greek word for "trophy"—an apt name considering the shape of the nasturtium flower and leaf.)

Eliminating Aphids

Try planting nasturtiums with fruits and vegetables susceptible to aphids. According to some organic gardeners, the aphids will gather on the nasturtiums, keeping fruits and vegetables aphid-free and providing you with an easier cleanup.

VALERIAN
(GARDEN HELIOTROPE)
Valeriana officinalis

Zones: 3–9

Type: Perennial

Light: Full sun

Size: 3–5 ft. tall,
4 ft. wide

Interest: Pink, white,
or lavender flowers in
4-inch-wide, fragrant
clusters

Uses: Aromatic, deco-
rative, medicinal

This fleshy herb, a favorite selection in old-fashioned gardens, forms an attractive clump of basal leaves, topped by tall stems with 2- to 4-inch flower clusters. Gardeners enjoy the sweet fragrance of valerian's pink, white, or lavender flowers. Valerian's aromatic roots drive felines wild but have a sedative effect on people. Oil extracted from valerian roots is used to season tobacco and add flavor to liqueurs, beers, and soft drinks. This herb works well at the back of perennial borders, in rock gardens, or when naturalized as part of a wildflower meadow. The leaves are divided into seven to ten leaflet pairs. While the sweet scent of valerian flowers is reminiscent of heliotrope (thus the common name, garden heliotrope), the rest of the plant, especially the roots, is somewhat malodorous, smelling like old socks to most people.

HOW TO GROW

Valerian thrives in rich, moist, well-drained soil in full sun. It tolerates both acidic and alkaline soils. Propagate from seeds in spring, covering seeds lightly with soil. (The germination rate may be as low as 50 percent of the seeds planted.) Propagate by dividing plants every three years in spring from Zone 6 north, and fall from Zone 7 south. Valerian rhizomes spread quickly, forming new plants, which can be lifted and moved elsewhere in the garden. If older clumps have begun to decline, invigorate the plants by dividing.

HOW TO USE

An effective tranquilizer, valerian is a popular over-the-counter remedy in Europe. Valerian tea calms the mind and alleviates insomnia, nervous headaches, upset stomachs, and hysteria. The tea, which tastes bitter but is soothing, is best brewed from fall-harvested rhizomes; use ½ teaspoon of dried ground root per cup of boiling water. Sweeten the tea with honey or sugar for improved flavor. Valerian in the bathwater may have a soothing effect.

CAUTION: *While a little valerian (a cup of tea per day) may be helpful, more may be toxic. In large quantities, valerian may cause agitation, headaches, and stupor.*

Top Choices

- V. 'Alba' has upright stems up to 4 feet tall decorated with white flowers in summer.

- V. 'Rubra' reaches 5 feet tall and has attractive red blossoms.

CATS LOVE IT

As appealing as catnip is to cats, valerian seems to have an even greater effect, driving felines into frenzied behaviors after just a few sniffs. The almost repulsive aroma of the dried root (it is nicknamed the Phew Plant) seems to be especially enticing.

Some sensitive cats are actually drawn to the scent of valerian in herbal teas. They can create a considerable mess scampering over tabletops and overturning trash cans in search of spent tea bags; take care to remove the temptation by discarding tea bags promptly.

EARTHWORMS LOVE IT TOO!

Planted in the garden, valerian lures beneficial earthworms, which are rapidly drawn to its phosphorus-rich roots. Grow it in different spots around the vegetable garden to promote their helpful presence. 🐛

FLANNEL MULLEIN
Verbascum thapsus

Zones: 5–9

Type: Biennial

Light: Full sun

Size: 2–6 ft. tall, 2 ft. wide

Interest: Tall spike of yellow flowers with a rosette of velvety gray-green leaves

Uses: Decorative, medicinal

Whether in the garden or by the road, flannel mullein has a presence few plants can challenge. Its towering height lends architectural interest and its dramatic appearance gives it enormous visual power, making it an excellent choice as an accent plant. Mullein produces a basal rosette of 6- to 9-inch-long, felted, gray-green leaves from which rises a strong, 6-foot-tall flower stalk. The woolly stem leaves are smaller and lead to a long flower spike studded with 1-inch-wide, five-petaled yellow flowers.

HOW TO GROW
Flannel mullein grows best in poor, dry, well-drained soil in full sun. Propagate from seeds in spring or fall, or from root cuttings in late winter or spring. If you prefer a mass planting rather than a single specimen,

set the plants about 2 to 3 feet apart. In its first year, flannel mullein grows a basal rosette of gray-green leaves. The next year, its flower stem rises up to 6 feet. If the stalk is not cut back after blooming, it may self-sow prolifically, producing large crops of easily transplanted seedlings. The soft, feltlike leaves may be subject to caterpillar attack, and in dry climates they get dusty and look a little worn out by summer's end.

HOW TO USE

Mullein looks terrific in groups at the back of a sunny border. A single plant makes a strong impact in front. Because it thrives in dry conditions, it also does well on slopes. A tea made with 1 teaspoon dried or 3 teaspoons fresh leaves or flowers steeped in 1 cup boiling water may help lung problems and act as a mild tranquilizer and pain reliever. (Tea from the leaves has a pungent taste, while flower tea is sweet.)

CAUTION: Do not ingest any mullein tea or decoction without first straining it to remove the downy hairs, which can irritate the throat.

Top Choices

- *V. chaixii* 'Album', chaix mullein, has white flowers with rosy stamens packed on its narrow, columnar stems. The woolly gray-green foliage has netted veins.

- *V. bombyciferum* 'Polar Summer' has large, fuzzy, silvery leaves and spikes of bright yellow summertime flowers on strong 4-foot-tall stems.

THE HISTORY OF FLANNEL

Both mullein's common name, flannel, and its genus name, *Verbascum*, refer to the thick covering of white hairs on the leaves.

Flannel mullein was brought to this country as a garden plant. It had several household uses in early American life.

- The stalks were dipped in tallow and lit for torches and wicks, giving rise to another common name, candlewick.

- American colonists tucked the soft leaves in their stockings for warmth. Native Americans stuck them in their moccasins for the same purpose.

- An infusion of mullein flowers has been used since Roman times as a rinse for blonde hair.

Candlelike stalks of bright yellow blossoms tower above the soft gray-green foliage of the flannel mullein plant.

VERVAIN
Verbena

Zones: 4–8

Type: Perennial

Light: Full sun

Size: 1–3 ft. tall,
2 ft. wide

Interest: Tiny purplish
flowers on narrow
spikes and deeply
divided basal leaves

Uses: Medicinal

Vervain's unassuming appearance belies powerful medicinal qualities. This spiky herb has four-angled stems that grow thick, upright, and sturdy at the base, and taper toward the pliant flowering tips. The terminal flower spikes branch on all sides, with one spike set above the others. Lower pinnate leaves are coarse in appearance, while the upper ones are small and, for the most part, entire. The little, pale mauve flowers have five lobes and four stamens. Native to Europe and parts of Asia and Africa, vervain has naturalized on roadsides and wastelands from Massachusetts south to Florida.

HOW TO GROW
Vervain is carefree and easy to grow. It thrives in full sun and rich, moist, well-drained soil but will adjust to many other conditions. Pinch the stem tips to stimulate

branching. Propagate vervain by sowing seeds in early spring or fall, dividing the roots in spring, or taking stem cuttings in late summer.

HOW TO USE

The entire plant contains medicinal properties that peak when the flowers just begin to bloom, usually early July. This is the perfect time to harvest the plant and dry it for later use. Some herbalists believe that vervain tea, made by steeping 1 teaspoon of dried herb in a cup of boiling water, can relieve indigestion, insomnia, coughs, nervousness, jaundice, and menstrual problems.

Taking a vervain bath is a traditional way to relieve tension and soothe the nerves. Make an infusion by pouring 3 cups of boiling water over ½ cup of dried vervain and steeping for 15 minutes. Pour the strained infusion into your bath and relax. As an alternative, fill a small cloth sack with ½ cup of dried herb, tie the bag closed, and place it in the tub while you fill it with warm water. You can keep the sack in the tub while you bathe.

Top Choice

- *V. hastata*, blue vervain, is native to wetlands and stream banks of North America. It bears small clusters of light blue flowers on 3- to 4-foot stems in summer. Some plants bear white or pink flowers. Zones 3 to 8.

VERVAIN MYTHS AND LEGENDS

Vervain's magical powers are the stuff of legends. Sacred in the Celtic and Germanic cultures and to ancient Egyptians, Persians, Romans, and Druids, the plant was frequently used in sacrificial rites. It was widely believed to bestow eternal life.

Medieval sorcerers and witches made love potions with vervain, which they believed to be a potent aphrodisiac. Worn around the neck, it brought good luck and protected the wearer from evil.

Legend holds that vervain grew on Mount Calvary and was gathered to stop the bleeding from Jesus' crucifixion wounds.

COST-EFFECTIVE CUTTING

To turn a single vervain plant into several, cut a 4-inch piece from the tip of each of several new shoots. Remove the lower leaves and dip the cut end into hormone rooting powder. Plant in a pot filled with well-drained soil mix and place in a bright, humid area. Tug on the plant periodically. When it offers some resistance, transplant the cutting into a new container filled with potting soil.

SWEET VIOLET
Viola odorata

Zones: 4–9

Type: Perennial

Light: Full sun to shade, depending on climate

Size: 4–6 in. tall, 12 in. wide

Interest: Fragrant flowers in purple, white, or lavender with dark green, heart-shaped leaves

Uses: Culinary, decorative, medicinal

One of about five hundred species of violas, sweet violet is especially appreciated for its beauty, sweet scent, and association with love. The plant is as useful as it is romantic and beautiful. The flowers and leaves can be used in everything from salads to medicinal teas and fragrant bouquets. The cheerful blossoms are nice additions to herb gardens or along perennial borders. The heart-shaped leaves are dark green with toothed margins. A tuft of violets sends out runners that in turn become new rooted clumps. Moreover, sweet violets also self-sow, resulting in new seedlings each spring.

HOW TO GROW
To encourage full, lavish clumps of lovely foliage, grow violets in part shade in rich, moist, humus-rich soil amended with plenty of compost. If you really favor the flowers,

play tough with your violets by providing drier and less fertile accommodations. Cutting back clumps in fall ensures a handsome fresh mound of foliage in spring. Propagate from seeds or by division in the spring. If planted near a lawn, sweet violet will spread into it. It also makes a good ground cover.

HOW TO USE

Violets make pretty, sweet-smelling cut flowers for nosegays and strewing. Harvest the flowers when first open, remove the stems, and enjoy them fresh or dry them for later use. Add fresh flowers to fruit and green salads, float them in drinks and punch bowls, or candy them for dessert decorations (see page 23). Dry in warm, dry shade to preserve their color and, for a short time, their fragrance for potpourris and flower crafts. Make a medicinal, calming tea from flowers or the leaves. A compress of crushed leaves may reduce swelling, while the roots and flowers have a cleansing, laxative effect. The violet-colored flowers also yield a purple dye.

Top Choices

- *V.* 'Rosina' has abundant quantities of fragrant pink to rose blossoms.

- *V.* 'Royal Robe' has fragrant, deep violet blossoms on 6-inch stems. Flowers are produced in spring with a repeat in fall.

- *V.* 'White Czar' has large white flowers that blossom in spring.

- *V. tricolor,* Johnny-jump-up, grows about 15 inches tall. Its winsome little pansylike flowers have three-colored faces of purple, yellow, and white.

NAPOLEON'S EMBLEM

Napoleon Bonaparte had a liking for sweet violets. He regarded them as a symbol of his affection for his wife, Josephine, and later took them to signify his reign as Emperor of France. When he was exiled, he vowed to return to France with the violet—a reference to his expectation to regain control of the government the following spring.

Napoleon did return to France with the violets but was defeated at the battle of Waterloo and again sent into exile. The following year, and every year since, the violets of France have consistently bloomed without him.

Johnny-jump-ups add a cheerful aspect to the spring garden and make a subtly flavored herb tea.

YUCCA
Yucca filamentosa

Zones: 5–10

Type: Perennial

Light: Full sun

Size: 2–3 ft. tall
(foliage); 5–6 ft. tall
(flowers); 5–6 ft. wide

Interest: Stiff, sword-
like foliage with an
upright, branched
spike of large, white,
bell-shaped flowers

Uses: Decorative,
medicinal

Yucca's bold, evergreen, sword-shaped leaves are 1 to 2 inches wide and 2 to 3 feet long, with sharp points and curly threads along the edges. The tall central flower stem has a panicle of white, waxy, drooping flowers, each measuring 2 to 3 inches across. The flowers, which have six petals and six stamens, are followed by large, woody pods suitable for dried flower arrangements. Yucca spreads slowly by offshoots consisting of similar rosettes with the characteristic sword-shaped leaves. It looks outstanding massed in an arid garden or used singly as a focal point in a flower bed or border.

HOW TO GROW
This slow-growing, adaptable plant, a member of the agave family, thrives in poor, dry soil and tolerates cold winters, hot and humid summers, and windy conditions.

Native to the semidesert areas of the southwestern United States, through the Southeast and along the Atlantic Coast from Rhode Island to Mexico, yucca needs well-drained soil. The only place it doesn't do well is a wet, shady site.

Propagate from root cuttings or by separating rooted offsets from the base of the plant and transplanting them to new locations. Remove old flower stalks and dead leaves before new growth begins in spring.

HOW TO USE

In the landscape, yucca's architectural quality harmonizes with diverse settings ranging from building foundations to perennial gardens and grassy or rocky banks. With its evergreen foliage and dramatic flower stalk, yucca is stunning as a container plant. Like Native Americans, you can use yucca's sturdy, pliant fibers to weave baskets, or double-boil the shoots to make a stimulating tonic. Mashing the roots in water releases the natural saponins (lathering agents) to make homemade soap or shampoo. Collect yucca's large, woody fruit pods in fall for dried flower arrangements.

Top Choices

- Y. 'Bright Edge' has variegated leaves striped with white and green.
- Y. 'Golden Sword' is another variegated variety with yellow-striped leaves creating a bright and beautiful accent in the garden.

GETTING YUCCA THROUGH THE WINTER

Most of the time, yucca is an easy-to-grow plant. Some winters, however, present a real challenge to its hardiness.

In Zones 5 and 6, the plants do best under a covering of snow for most of winter. During years when little snow falls, the plants may suffer browning of the leaf edges and tips.

To be sure your yucca plant comes through winter in the best possible condition, cover the leaves with a layer of straw after the ground freezes. Cover the straw with a layer of pine boughs for adequate overwinter protection.

YUCCA IN THE HERB GARDEN

The bold leaves and flower stalks of yucca are complemented by the relaxed habit and muted tones of other herbs. Interplant it with summer savory, garden sage, English lavender, and thyme, herbs that can tolerate the same soil conditions as yucca.

Harvesting & Preserving Herbs

When to Harvest

Harvesting herbs is not a difficult thing to do. A snip here and there yields plenty of basil, thyme, and many other herbs. The trick to harvesting is not so much the method as the timing. Many herbs rely on volatile oils for their flavor and aroma; the concentrations of these oils change over time. To harvest the best-tasting herbs, you must gather them when the oils are at their peak. Oil content changes over the course of the growing season as well as over the course of each day.

As a general rule, herbs grown for their leaves, such as basil and rosemary, are most potent from the time flower buds form to when the buds begin to open. Biennial herbs, including parsley, are best before any flower stalk appears. Harvest leafy herbs in the morning when the leaves are dry but before they are in direct sunlight.

Flowers, such as daylilies and violets, are most flavorful when the blossoms are about three-quarters open. Herbs grown for their roots, such as purple coneflower, are most potent in fall after the plant has flowered and finished its yearly growth.

Preserving Herbs by Drying

There are many methods of drying herbs, ranging from ancient to high-tech. All are worth a try, depending on your needs and facilities. Some preserve more flavor and color than others.

Air Drying
Air drying is an ancient method of preserving herbs and is a good method for preparing large amounts of leaves. To air-dry, gather the herb into bunches of from five to seven stems each. Tie the bunches with twine or string and hang them upside down in a warm, dimly lit room. Leave enough space between bundles so the herbs do not touch. If the air is

humid, use a fan to increase air circulation and reduce the chance of mold forming on the leaves. Check the plants frequently. When dry, crumble them and store in lidded glass jars in a cool, dimly lit place.

Air drying is easy to do and an excellent method of preparing plants for dried arrangements. The herbs do lose some flavor, and plants left hanging too long can become moldy, dusty, or tasteless.

Oven Drying

Oven drying is an option for drying herbs where space is limited. Spread the leaves or roots in a single layer on a cookie sheet and place in the oven. The pilot light on gas ovens provides just enough heat to dry the herbs slowly and evenly. Fluff the herbs once or twice a day while they dry—usually for a period of three to five days. If using an electric oven, set it on warm and leave the door ajar. Check herbs daily, turning the oven off at night and re-setting in the morning—until the herbs are dry. Oven drying is satisfactory for small amounts of herbs but can rob the leaves of flavor. It also is not energy-efficient. This method is excellent for preparing roots, however.

Microwave Drying

Microwave drying takes only brief amounts of time to produce a high-quality product. This method does require frequent monitoring, and only small amounts of an herb can be dried at any one time. Place a layer of paper towels on a microwave-safe pie plate. After gathering the herb, spread the leaves in a single layer on the pie plate. Be sure the leaves are dry and free of all surface moisture; wet leaves will cook instead of dry. Microwave on high for 1 to 3 minutes, checking the plants after each minute. The herb is "done" when the leaves feel dry to the touch and have not lost any color. The pie plate also heats up during this process and must cool down before being reused. Allow the herb to cool. Store in an airtight glass jar.

Cool-Air Drying

Cool-air drying is another name for refrigerator drying, a technique that has become very popular over the last few years. It produces very high-quality results and retains excellent flavor and color. Cool-air drying can be done only in frost-free refrigerators. It works best for leaves, flower petals, and herbs that lose flavor quickly, such as dill and parsley. To cool-air-dry herbs, lay paper towels on a cookie sheet. Spread a single layer of the herb on the paper towels and place in the refrigerator. If space is at a premium, place the herbs in an onion bag. Hang the bag from a magnetic hook attached to the inside of the refrigerator. Check the herbs daily for dryness. In cool weather, the herbs should be dry in about a week, while in hot weather, drying can take as little as three days. Store the dried herbs in lidded glass jars.

Cool-air drying is useful for preparing small quantities of herbs. It does not work in crisper bins. (In theory, this technique should work well in frost-free freezers as well as frost-free refrigerators, but it doesn't.)

Dehydrator Drying

Electric dehydrators are designed to dry food by circulating heated (105° to 115° F) air over and around the food. Most manufacturers supply directions for drying herbs, which eliminates a great deal of experimentation. Most herbs dried in a dehydrator retain good flavor and color. Some, such as basil, lose too much flavor using this method. Knowing which herbs to dry in a dehydrator and which to process in other ways does require a bit of experimentation. An advantage to dehydrator drying is that the herbs do not require monitoring; just turn on the unit and wait. Dehydrators are not large appliances, so the amount of herbs you can dry in each batch is limited.

Freezing Herbs

Freezing herbs is fast and easy but it is not a good method for everything. Freezing damages the cells of plants and as a result, frozen herbs often become soft and mushy when thawed. This does not matter if the herbs are used in cooking, but do not expect frozen herbs to make a good garnish. Some herbs have a nasty habit of turning black in the freezer; preserve these by drying or pureeing then freezing. The puree will not turn black. The best herbs to freeze include dill, mint, and rosemary.

To freeze herbs, spread individual sprigs on a small tray or aluminum pie plate and place in the freezer overnight. The next day, remove the herbs and store in labeled freezer bags. Refreeze. Remove individual sprigs or leaves as you need them. Reseal and return the bag to the freezer.

Glossary

Acidic soil: Soil with a pH value of less than 7.0.

Alkaline soil: Soil with a pH value of more than 7.0.

Annual: A plant that completes its life cycle (germination, flowering, seed production, and death) in one growing season.

Axil: The notchlike angle formed by the union of the leaf stem (petiole) and the plant stem.

Basal leaf: A leaf that grows from the base of a plant.

Basal rosette: A cluster of leaves at the base of a plant.

Biennial: A plant that completes its life cycle (germination, flowering, seed production, and death) in two growing seasons.

Blade: The broad, flat portion of a leaf.

Bolting: The rapid growth of a flower stalk; usually refers to annuals and biennials.

Bract: Leaves at the base of a flower that are different in shape, form, or texture from other leaves on the plant.

Compound leaf: A leaf with two or more leaflets attached to the central leaf stalk.

Cultivar: A composite of "cultivated variety"; a distinct plant form maintained only through vegetative reproduction or inbred seeds.

Cutting: A plant portion that is removed from the parent plant and treated to regrow stems, roots, or leaves to become a self-sustaining plant.

Deadheading: The removal of spent flowers to encourage additional flower bud formation or discourage seed formation.

Deciduous: Describing a plant that sheds all its leaves at some time during the year.

Disk flower: The round, central portion of a daisylike flower, composed of many very small, tubular flowers.

Division: Propagation achieved by cutting one clump of a plant into smaller pieces that then become individual plants. Also, a new plant that has been created by this method.

Double flower: A blossom with more petals than normal.

Evergreen: Describing a plant that does not shed its leaves at any time during the year. Also, a plant having this characteristic.

Everlasting: A plant or flower, such as curry plant, that retains much of its color and form after being gathered and dried.

Family: A group of closely related genera, such as grasses or legumes.

Genus: A group of closely related species. (Plural: genera)

Glaucous: Having a powdery coating or a grayish color.

Graft: A method of propagation in which a shoot of one plant is removed and joined to a another plant, called a rootstock, or stock.

Habit: A plant's distinctive, natural shape, such as spreading or conical.

Humus: Soil portion composed of partially decomposed organic matter. You can purchase or create humus to add to soil.

Keel: A raised ridge along a portion of a plant, such as a leaf, flower, fruit, or stem.

Leaflet: One of the divisions of a compound leaf.

Margin: The edge of a leaf.

Node: The points along the stem where buds develop, singly or in groups.

Obovate: A leaf whose blade is broader above the center. The opposite of ovate.

Ovate: A leaf whose blade is broader below the center.

Organic matter: Material derived from decomposed remains of plants and animals; includes manure and leaves.

Panicle: An open, usually pyramidal, cluster of flowers.

Perennial: A plant that survives for three or more years.

Petiole: The stalk that attaches the leaf to the stem of a plant.

pH: The scale used to measure the concentration of hydrogen ions in a solution, which controls how acidic or alkaline the solution is. The pH scale runs from 0 to 14, with 7.0 being neutral. Any value less than 7.0 is acidic and any value exceeding 7.0 is alkaline. In horticulture, pH most often refers to the measure of soil acidity.

Pinnate: Having leaflets arranged in two rows along a central leaf stalk.

Propagation: The technique of producing more plants.

Ray flower: The petal-like portion arranged symmetrically around a central disk of a composite flower, such as a daisy.

Rhizome: A horizontal underground stem that is sometimes thin, as in mint, and sometimes enlarged, as in iris, to serve as a storage organ for starches and other carbohydrates—an energy source for spring sprouting.

Rosette: A cluster of leaves.

Runner: A slender, aboveground stem that produces a new plant at its terminal end.

Scape: A leafless flower stalk that rises from the ground, as in daylilies.

Single flower: A flower with the normal number of petals for its species.

Species: A group of very closely related plants.

Stock: The parent plant from which propagation material, such as cuttings, is taken.

Stamen: The male portion of a flower, consisting of the filament and the anther, which contains the pollen.

Sucker: A shoot that rises from buds along the roots. As these shoots grow, they form their own roots. Suckers can then be separated from the parent plant and transplanted.

Taproot: The long, usually thick root grown by some plants, such as carrots. Taproots often serve as storage organs and have few branching roots. Many plants that produce taproots are difficult to transplant.

Toothed: Having small lobes along the margins of leaves, flowers, or other parts of a plant.

Two-lipped: Divided into upper and lower sections, usually in reference to the flowers of plants in the mint family.

Umbel: A flower cluster with floral stems that radiate from a central point, as in dill.

Variegated: Having streaked or blotched coloration, other than green, on plant parts such as leaves or flowers; caused by cellular mutations that disrupt the normal production of chlorophyll.

Whorl: A group of three or more leaves that rise from a single node.

Zone Map

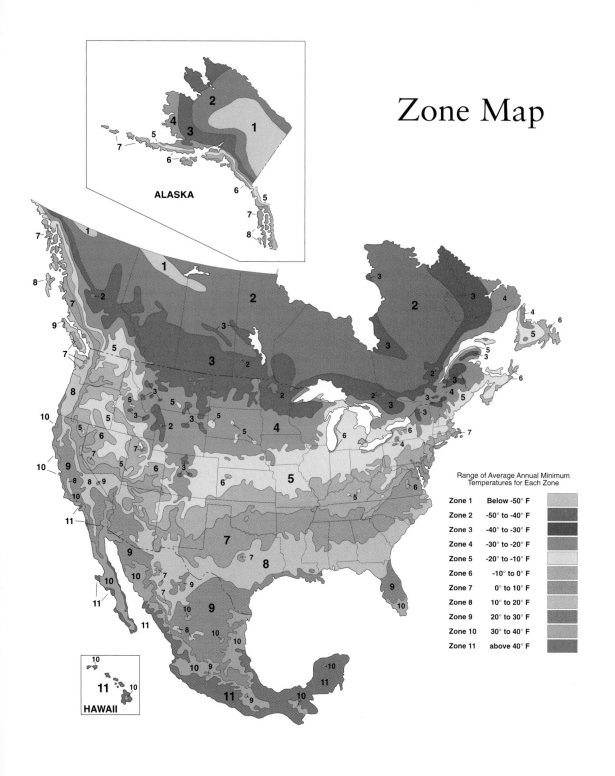

ALASKA

HAWAII

Range of Average Annual Minimum
Temperatures for Each Zone

Zone 1	Below -50° F
Zone 2	-50° to -40° F
Zone 3	-40° to -30° F
Zone 4	-30° to -20° F
Zone 5	-20° to -10° F
Zone 6	-10° to 0° F
Zone 7	0° to 10° F
Zone 8	10° to 20° F
Zone 9	20° to 30° F
Zone 10	30° to 40° F
Zone 11	above 40° F

Photography & Illustration Credits

David Cavagnaro
60, 106 and 107

Rosalind Creasy
72

Thomas E. Eltzroth
16, 26, 40, 54 and 96

Derek Fell
Front Cover, Title Page, 32, 36, 46, 62, 64, 70, 76, 85, 88, 108 and 110

Bill Johnson
87 and 111

Susan Berry Langsten, Illustrator
13, 15, 41, 47, 57A, 57B, 81A, 81B, 91, 93, 99A, 99B, 101A and 101B

Marla Murphy
8

Jerry Pavia,
Jerry Pavia Photography, Inc.
14, 20, 24, 34, 52, 56, 66, 80, 98, 100 and 102

Richard Shiell
9, 10, 18, 48, 78, 92 and 112

Steven M. Still
86 and 104

Joseph G. Strauch, Jr.
12, 22, 28, 30, 38, 42, 44, 50, 58, 68, 74, 82, 84, 90 and 94

INDEX

*Page numbers in italics refer
to illustrations.*

Storey Communications, Inc.
Pownal, Vermont

President: M. John Storey
Executive Vice President: Martha M. Storey
Chief Operating Officer: Dan Reynolds
Director of Custom Publishing: Deirdre Lynch
Project Manager: Barbara Weiland
Author: Penny O'Sullivan
Book Design: Betty Kodela
Design Assistance: Jen Rork
Horticultural Review: Charly W. G. Smith